Representation
and Design

SUNY Series in Medieval Studies
Paul E. Szarmach, Editor

Representation
and Design

Tracing a Hermeneutics of
Old English Poetry

Pauline E. Head

State University of New York Press

Published by
State University of New York Press, Albany

© 1997 State University of New York

For information, address State University of New York
Press, State University Plaza, Albany, N.Y., 12246

Production by Diane Ganeles
Marketing by Bernadette LaManna

Library of Congress Cataloging-in-Publication Data

Head, Pauline E., 1954–
    Representation and design : tracing a hermeneutics of Old English
poetry / Pauline E. Head.
        p.   cm. — (SUNY series in medieval studies)
    Includes bibliographical references and index.
    ISBN 0-7914-3203-3 (alk. paper). — ISBN 0-7914-3204-1 (pbk. :
alk. paper)
    1. English literature—Old English, ca. 450–1100—History and
criticism—Theory, etc.   2. Authors and readers—England—History.
3. Reader-response criticism.   4. Mimesis in literature.
5. Rhetoric, Medieval.   6. Hermeneutics.   I. Title.   II. Series.
PR201.H43   1997
829.09—dc20   96-2391
                                                                  CIP

10 9 8 7 6 5 4 3 2 1

To Rick and Nicholas

Contents

Illustrations

1. Oxford Bodleian MS Junius 11 (The Junius Manuscript), p. 11. God in heaven, Adam and Eve in paradise. Reprinted by permission of The Bodleian Library, Oxford.
2. Oxford Bodleian MS Junius 11 (The Junius Manuscript), p. 13. Adam and Eve in paradise. Reprinted by permission of The Bodleian Library, Oxford.
3. Oxford Bodleian MS Junius 11 (The Junius Manuscript), p. 73. Noah and family leaving ark. Reprinted by permission of The Bodleian Library, Oxford.
4. Oxford Bodleian MS Junius 11 (The Junius Manuscript), p. 9. God putting Adam to sleep and creating Eve. Angels in heaven. Reprinted by permission of The Bodleian Library, Oxford.
5. Oxford Bodleian MS Junius 11 (The Junius Manuscript), p. 44. Sentencing of Adam and Eve. Reprinted by permission of The Bodleian Library, Oxford.
6. Oxford Bodleian MS Junius 11 (The Junius Manuscript), p. 20. Satan sending messenger who tempts Eve. Reprinted by permission of The Bodleian Library, Oxford.
7. Oxford Bodleian MS Junius 11 (The Junius Manuscript), p. 36. The messenger returning to Satan. Reprinted by permission of The Bodleian Library, Oxford.
8. Ruthwell Cross, north face. Christ on the Beasts. Copyright: Department of Archaeology, University of Durham. Photograph by T. Middlemass.
9. Ruthwell Cross, lower section of west face. Runic inscription and vinescroll. Copyright: Department of Archaeology, University of Durham. Photograph by T. Middlemass.
10. Trinity College Dublin MS 57 (The Book of Durrow), fol. 191v. Symbol of St. John. Reprinted by permission of The Board of Trinity College Dublin.

Acknowledgments

My work on *Representation and Design* began when I was a doctoral student at the Centre for Medieval Studies, University of Toronto. I would like to thank the members of my thesis committee, whose various responses to my writing were instructive, thought-provoking, and encouraging: Ashley Crandell Amos, Roberta Frank, Allen Frantzen, Linda Hutcheon, Michael Sheehan, Brian Stock, and David Townsend. To Roberta Frank, my thesis supervisor, who has guided this project from the beginning with thoughtful and valuable advice, I am particularly grateful; the generous time and attention she has given to matters both conceptual and practical is very much appreciated. I am especially thankful as well to Brian Stock; our many discussions about my work were immeasurably important to the development of my ideas. Recalling consultations with Ashley and with Father Sheehan renews the feeling of loss I share with many others at their deaths; I was very fortunate to have had the opportunity to exchange ideas with such knowledgeable and thoughtful scholars.

My research has benefited greatly from the resources at the Dictionary of Old English project, and I have appreciated the constant interest my friends at the Dictionary have expressed in my work. My colleagues at York University, Ross Arthur and Ian Balfour especially, have been supportive and generous in providing advice. The instructive criticisms of James Earl and the comments of several other, anonymous readers for SUNY Press were of great value during my final revisions. I am grateful to Carola Sautter and Diane Ganeles of SUNY Press for their patient and professional guidance through the publishing process. This book has been written with the support of an Ontario Graduate Scholarship and a Social Sciences and Humanities Research Council grant; costs of production were in part funded by a research grant from the Faculty of Arts, York University, for which I am grateful.

Introduction

In the literary criticism of the last several decades, there has been a shift from an author-centered method of interpretation to one that acknowledges the participation of the reader with the text in the construction of meanings. A written text is no longer imagined to be a representation of an individual's perception of reality, a work centered somewhere between an authorial production and a reader's reception, and transcendent of cultural difference. Instead, it can now be understood as a place where many writings and readings converge. When the text is decentered and its plurality of (sometimes contradictory) meanings recognized, questions arise regarding interpretive methods; the complexity of processes of reading are acknowledged. There is no one ideal and correct way of reading; differences within and between cultures produce varying interpretive practices.[1]

Almost thirty years ago, Barthes described a text as "a tissue of quotations drawn from innumerable centres of culture," and said that the writer "can only imitate a gesture that is always anterior, never original. His only power is to mix writings, to counter the ones with the others in such a way as never to rest on any one of them."[2] This reconceptualization of the text is immediately relevant to readers of Old English poetry, given the formulaic, repetitive structures of verse composition, the anonymity of almost all the poetry, and our inability to date much of the corpus more precisely than within several centuries—but, until very recently, studies of the literature had not responded to recent critical approaches.[3] *Beowulf* and *The Wanderer* continued to be read as if they were modern novels, the former casually referred to as representative of its eighth-century environment, and the latter defined as depicting the growth of an individual's character. An apparently more historical approach, but one that fell within the same preconceptual framework, was that of constructing a genealogy wherein Old English texts took their place according to their ancestors and

1

descendents.[4] Barthes's critique of source hunting, in another essay, is again so appropriate that it could have been written with Old English poetry in mind: "To try to find the 'sources,' the 'influences,' of a work, is to fall in with the myth of filiation; the citations which go to make up the text are anonymous, untraceable, and yet *already read*: they are quotations without inverted commas."[5] The constant, variable formulae that play a part in the construction of an Old English poem are precisely "anonymous," "untraceable," unpunctuated quotations; the poem has no author, no one individual responsible for creating its unique existence in reference to other works.[6]

Horizons and Frames

In this study, I examine the poetry from the point of view of its reception, speculatively describing its reading by an Anglo-Saxon audience but also drawing on modes of interpretation available to me—all reader-oriented interpretation is more or less self-reflexive. Since the idea of a single correct way of reading is a fiction even with regard to the way a particular culture approaches its texts, I take as my starting point the assumption that Anglo-Saxon concepts of reading were probably very different from those that have dominated our own literary culture. Attempting to trace an Anglo-Saxon hermeneutics involves deriving a theory from the texts themselves; there are no contemporary (i.e., Anglo-Saxon) manuals of vernacular poetics, no discourse writes about the poetry describing its method of signifying. Although I shall not be examining parallels between Old English poetry and Christian Latin literature, that particular route to a contextual understanding of the poetry's signification has much to offer and has been followed in recent scholarship.[7] I turn instead to Anglo-Saxon pictorial and poetic texts for evidence, not treating them as objects—with the pretense of detachment and objectivity—but conceiving of them as reflections of interpretive practice.

Before describing my interests and methods more precisely, some consideration of this project's conceptual framework is necessary. When I speak of tracing a hermeneutics of Old English poetry, I mean to imply a method of interpretation that resonates against Gadamer's "art of understanding" but at the same time rejects, through its provisional "tracing," his belief in a final moment of comprehension. Gadamer conceptualizes reading as a "fusion of horizons":

> We started by saying that a hermeneutical situation is determined by the prejudices that we bring with us. They constitute, then, the horizon of a

particular present, for they represent that beyond which it is impossible to see. But now it is important to avoid the error of thinking that it is a fixed set of opinions and evaluations that determine and limit the horizon of the present, and that the otherness of the past can be distinguished from it as from a fixed ground. . . . There is no more an isolated horizon of the present than there are historical horizons. Understanding, rather, is always the fusion of these horizons which we imagine to exist by themselves.[8]

If the reader's horizon (that of a "particular present") is fluid and joins with the horizon of the text ("the otherness of the past"), which is also permeable, there can be no clear distinction between the reader as subject and the text as object. Gadamer says this in a very concise, provocative way: "understanding belongs to the being of that which is understood" (p. xix). Active and passive participles indicating the process and product of interpretation reflect each other and then merge in their signification, so that neither can have a separate existence; this circularity perplexes a logic of binarism. The false pursuit and pretense of "objective" reading is undermined by such a reconceptualization of the process of understanding, and "prejudice" is reformed into a necessary and productive element of this process.

In my writing, I acknowledge my own particular late twentieth-century frame of reference and introduce it to my reading of late tenth-century manuscripts, not imagining the texts as objects for my impartial scrutiny. In addition, though, I propose that such a merging of subject and object positions characterizes a complex Anglo-Saxon mode of interpretation. This is especially apparent in the hermeneutics suggested by the Old English riddles, wherein objects (or creatures, e.g., a horn, a bow, or a magpie) cast themselves as speaking subjects, overstepping their existential limits. The interpreter of these poems must identify *with* the objects in order to identify them. As a subject, the speaker is like the reader; it performs human actions and speaks about its performance. Simultaneously, the reader approaches the speaker (aligns her or his view with its) and the speaker approaches the reader (shares her or his human attributes). The reader is never offered a distant, stable position from which to observe the object of her or his perception.

My use of the term "hermeneutics," then, has two, ultimately inseparable, references. It both indicates the methodology through which I interpret Anglo-Saxon reading practices and describes those reading practices themselves. In other words, my project in this book consists of my reading of Anglo-Saxon reading.

Gadamer's theories of interpretation have more than a general relevance to my attempt at "tracing a hermeneutics of Old English poetry"; his images of space and time bear on my own conceptualizations of interpretive perspectives (in chapter 1) and narrative temporality (in chapter 3). The notion of a "horizon" conjures a picture of a wide but limited space:

> The horizon is the range of vision that includes everything that can be seen from a particular vantage point. . . . A person who has no horizon is a man who does not see far enough and hence overvalues what is nearest to him. Contrariwise, to have a horizon means not to be limited to what is nearest, but to be able to see beyond it" (269).

Through this image, understanding is pictured as seeing and the recognition of prejudices as an ability to see beyond "what is nearest," but not to see limitless vistas. The reader's act of understanding is conceived of as being rooted in a particular situation that has a specific relation to the territory of the text. While placement is necessary—there can be no transcendence of historical limitation—the places of the two (reader and text) are not fixed: "The horizon is, rather, something into which we move and that moves with us. Horizons change for a person who is moving" (271). It is by "continually [testing] all our prejudices" (273) that we allow our horizons to be flexible. The act of reading involves tracing a tentative position in relation to the text, and then moving in response to its changing contours of signification.

In chapter 1, I theorize the problem of comprehending first-person speech in Old English poetry by considering the implications of perspective. The reader's project when confronted with poems such as *The Wanderer*, *The Dream of the Rood*, or many of the Exeter Book riddles can be described spatially: she or he must find a position in relation to the enigmatic speaker, in order to identify (with) the character and make the world of the text comprehensible. The difficulty of these texts necessitates an awareness of horizons, since to approach the poems means to question conventional notions of character and narrative. In *The Wanderer*, representation of speech and landscape are fragmentary, and the reader is disoriented (as witnessed by the numerous attempts of literary critics to fix the poem's speech boundaries). Turning to the pictorial art of the same period for a visual representation of perspective, a similar multiplicity of vantage points is apparent. The illustrations of Genesis in MS Junius 11 (Oxford, Bodleian Library; see figs. 1 to 7) do not describe for the viewer a precise physical position. Just as there is no one viewing position for the reader of these illuminations, there is no single narrative point of view available to the reader of *The Wanderer*. In chapter 1, I explore the implications of this analogy; Gadamer's spatial metaphor for the hermeneutic process, then, bears upon my reading of Anglo-Saxon representations of identity and perspective.

Another, related, concept fundamental to Gadamer's theories of interpretation is that of "effective history." The past is not simply a period of time that has ended, that is delineated absolutely from our present, only retrievable through assimilation:

> Historical consciousness is aware of its own otherness and hence distinguishes the horizon of tradition from its own. On the other hand, it is itself, as we are trying to show, only something laid over a continuing tradition, and hence it immediately recombines what it has distinguished in order, in the unity of the historical horizon that it thus acquires, to become again one with itself.
>
> The projecting of the historical horizon, then, is only a phase in the process of understanding, and does not become solidified into the self-alienation of a past consciousness, but is overtaken by our own present horizon of understanding. In the process of understanding there takes place a real fusing of horizons, which means that as the historical horizon is projected, it is simultaneously removed. We described the conscious act of this fusion as the task of effective-historical consciousness. (273–74)

In the interpretive process, past (the horizon of the past represented by the text) and present (the reader's horizon) are not distinct but are contained within a historical continuum. Distinguishing the "two" horizons is only a momentary gesture before understanding recognizes and recreates their union.

Gadamer's concept of historicity describes the present as circling back through and reintegrating the past, rather than moving away from it, shedding its "otherness." In chapter 3, I consider the relationship of past and present as represented in Old English poetry. The poetic manuscripts were inscribed within a culture in which written language held a central place, yet they bear traces of oral composition and transmission, reintroducing orality at the very moment of their transcription.

The poems, then, refer back to a prior mode of composition, and they do this both explicitly, through the restaging of storytelling situations, and structurally, through their nonlinear composition. New words were typically constructed by recasting existing vocabulary, so that past meanings would be renewed and altered in present language. Phrases and poetic themes would also be reshaped, deriving value and acquiring meaning through their repetition and versatility. The poems' narrative pacing, marked by interruptions and digressions, indicates that Anglo-Saxon storytelling was not primarily concerned with the unbroken representation of chronology. I interpret the poet's process of recollection and repetition as signifying continuity and the cyclic movement of time; reading or listening to the poetry, I suggest, would have involved a similar process of retrospection, recollection, awareness of the past. The written record (the manuscript poem) was one way of remembering, and it recalled another; a memory of storytelling inspired a narrative which, in turn, evoked a memory.

Old English poetry can be considered a reflection on the past. Like Gadamer's "horizon of the present," it carries its past with it rather than drawing on history as if from something distinct. Again, Gadamer's theory has a double implication in my work; my late twentieth-century method of reading this poetry is shaped by an attitude toward the past that is represented in the late tenth-century poetry. Gadamer speaks of echoes: "Our historical consciousness is always filled with a variety of voices in which the echo of the past is heard" (252). I attempt to trace a hermeneutics that is attentive to the resonance of the literature I am reading.

Yet I depart from Gadamer precisely regarding the ultimate end of these spatial and temporal movements, the moment when interpretive horizons finally merge. Although Gadamer rejects the idealism of objective analysis, in some of his writings he perpetuates an idealistic belief in a different kind of absolute understanding:

> When at last we have got to the bottom of something which seemed to us strange and unintelligible, when we have managed to accommodate it within our linguistically ordered world, then everything falls into place, just as it does with a difficult chess problem, where only the solution renders the necessity of the absurd setup intelligible, down to the very last piece on the board.[9]

As I argue in my readings of the riddles and *The Dream of the Rood* (in chapter 1), and narrative structure generally (in chapter 3), Old English poetry does not privilege an ultimate moment of accommodation and resolution, in light of which complexities and contradictions dissolve. Being attentive to these texts, it is appropriate to trace a hermeneutics in which horizons are constructed ad hoc and in which the reader's interest is in the process of constructing. Elsewhere Gadamer is less absolute: "The working out of the hermeneutical situation means the achievement of the right horizon of enquiry for the questions evoked by the encounter with tradition" (269). This seems to describe a dialogical situation, a conversation with the past within a certain constructed context. Yet "the *achievement* of the *right* horizon of enquiry" still lacks appropriate provisionality.

In chapter 2, I consider the significance of framing structures in Anglo-Saxon narrative and pictorial representation; Derrida's tracing of the implications of frames guides my reading. For the purposes of articulating my theoretical perspective—one that deviates from Gadamer's conclusiveness—I would like to superimpose Derrida's concept of the frame upon Gadamer's image of the horizon. In condensing the similarities and differences between the two philosophies of interpretation by concentrating on these very specific aspects, I intend to achieve no more than an image that clarifies the often implicit, theoretical stance of my own interpretive project. The bridges and gaps between the thinking of Gadamer and Derrida represent an interface between German hermeneutics and French deconstruction; in the words of Hugh Silverman, "The conjunction of semiotics and hermeneutics is a difficult space to occupy."[10] An extensive literature exists on this absorbing topic, a subject that must remain peripheral to my reading of Old English texts.[11]

A horizon is a natural visible and visual limit, created by the apparent fusion of sky and earth along a distant line. It is apparent to the perceiver whose outlook created it; the notion of a horizon, therefore, refers to sky and earth, but it always also looks back upon the perceiving subject. Its circularity contrasts with the angularity of a frame. The frame (e.g., a picture frame) is constructed in order to enhance what it surrounds by distinguishing its contents from the less important surroundings. The frame does not refer to the natural world but concerns both the text it delineates and the viewer's way of reading that text.

I do not mean to simplify the two concepts into opposing images; Gadamer uses the image of a "horizon" to describe a reading situation that is worked out, not explicitly to refer to a natural phenomenon, and Derrida allows for the possibility of a frame that is not angular.[12] By unpacking the implications of the terms *horizon* and *frame*, I intend to sketch a superimposition that suggests significant differences between the two hermeneutical theories. Both are spatial ways of conceiving interpretation that draw attention to necessary limits and thus, most basically, reject the reader's objectivity as well as the text's transcendency.

In "Parergon," Derrida explores Kant's third *Critique* concerning aesthetic judgment, following a circuitous route characterized by interrogation: "What is it about at bottom? The bottom" (38). In interpeting both Kant's construction of a frame for his argument and his explicit discussion of frames (*parerga*), Derrida plays with the possibility of articulating a "theory of the frame," a theory that all aesthetics presuppose but that has never existed: "Now you have to know what you're talking about, what *intrinsically* concerns the value "beauty" and what remains external to your immanent sense of beauty" (45). Kant describes parerga as "ornamentation, . . . i.e., what is only an adjunct, and not an intrinsic constituent in the complete representation of the object." This ornamentation augments "by means of its form"; "thus it is with the frames of pictures or the drapery on statues, or the colonnades of palaces" (53). Derrida has "great difficulties" with Kant's examples (63–64), and questions the margin since it is a place crucial to signification:

> *Parerga* have a thickness, a surface which separates them not only (as Kant would have it) from the integral inside, from the body proper of the *ergon*, but also from the outside, from the wall on which the painting is hung, from the space in which the statue or column is erected, then, step by step, from the whole field of historical, economic, political inscription in which the drive to signature is produced. . . . No 'theory,' no 'practice,' no 'theoretical practice' can intervene effectively in this field if it does not weigh up and bear on the frame, which is the decisive structure of what is at stake. (61)

Derrida's text, then, concerns the significance of the frame's interventions in both directions: in the text that has been placed inside and in everything else that has been relegated to the outside.

Horizons have no tangibility; whenever you move, or even shift your gaze, your horizon is affected. The limits described by the horizon are set by the vantage point of the observer on the object of her or his vision. Gadamer's primary reference, through this model, is to the perceiving subject, the reader. The frame, on the other hand, has "thickness"; it is attached to the text and has been placed just there by the author or the reader, or through their collaboration. Derrida theorizes the semantic relationship between frame and content, and questions exactly how—by what criteria—the reader differentiates the "two": "But this frame is problematical. I do not know what is essential and what is accessory in a work" (63). Gadamer, like Derrida, is concerned with circumstance when he speaks of achieving the right horizon of enquiry; this goal would have to be reached by excluding the irrelevant, thereby framing the relevant. He does not, however, problematize the placement of the delimitation; his horizon is not constituted (like a frame), but discovered and intelligently chosen. Gadamer's hermeneutics is characterized by confidence about beginnings and endings—about both the initial act of defining the right horizon and the final, conclusive achievement of understanding when the horizons of the reader and the text merge.[13] Besides describing a confidence about the temporal beginning and ending of the process of interpretation, his hermeneutics is optimistic concerning conceptual limits: whatever is irrelevant is cast beyond the limits of vision/understanding—it is out of sight—and "the relative significance of everything within this horizon" is known to the perceiver/interpreter (269).

Derrida's thoughts about limits are speculative and skeptical, and their circular, *mise en abyme* structure contributes to the subversion of any confidence about conceptual boundaries. In a preliminary discussion of Hegel's *Lectures on Aesthetics* and Heidegger's *Origin of the Work of Art*, he says of the two philosophers: "They both start out from a figure of the circle and they stay there. . . . Circle of circles, circle in the encircled circle. How could a circle place itself *en abyme?*" (23–24). Repetition chases away any stable referent; context is complicated as possible frames of reference encircle each other infinitely. From this starting point, he writes about Kant's framed text, which concerns frames, and asks the (already framed) question of the frame. Discourse about a topic is not distinct from the object of its enquiry, and beginnings and endings flow into each other, eluding conclusiveness.

An end of interpretation can be reached according to Gadamer's process: "When at last we have got to the bottom of something . . . everything falls into place"[14]; through Derrida's writing the expectation of any resolution circles back on itself: "What is it about at bottom? The bottom" (38). There is no solid fundament at the beginning of Derrida's interpretation either: "One must know—this is a fundamental presupposition, presupposing what is fundamental—how to determine the intrinsic—what is framed—and know what one is excluding as frame *and* outside-the-frame. We are thus *already* at the unlocatable center of the problem" (63). Although Gadamer's interpretive horizons are fluid and shifting, they eventually—if, perhaps, temporarily—settle at the moment when the reader's prejudicial context merges with the text's historical presence. Derrida's writing enacts a complex interpretation wherein frames of reference—sets of assumptions—are perpetually undermined and the stillness representative of understanding is never reached. He puts forward an "interpretation of interpretation . . . which is no longer turned to an origin," and which

> affirms play and tries to pass beyond man and humanism, the name of man being the name of that being who throughout the history of metaphysics or of onto-theology—in other words, throughout his entire history—has dreamed of full presence, the reassuring foundation, the origin, and the end of the play.[15]

Fred Dallmayr summarizes the oppositions arising from the exchange between Gadamer and Derrida in Paris, April 1981, as comprising: "Understanding versus non-understanding, immanence versus otherness, continuity versus rupture, truth versus non-truth."[16] While my interpretation of Anglo-Saxon reading practices is influenced by Gadamer's hermeneutics (in ways I have suggested above), I argue that, ultimately, Derrida's process of unsettling meaning is very appropriate to the enigmatic, structurally complex texts I am studying.

Throughout this book, I question the semantic roles of representation and design in Old English poetry. By these terms I imply and dispute the conventional dichotomy interpretation makes between content and form; content is redefined as representation—a reflection of texts and ideologies, form is recognized as complex and meaningful design, and any distinction between the "two" for the purposes of interpretation is drawn into question and disrupted. My discussion in chapter 2 explicitly concerns frames and, following Derrida, asks if Anglo-Saxon narrative and pictorial frames are purely formal. By looking at frames, I am questioning the signifying roles of visual and conceptual boundaries, as well as of design in a general sense. Frames—essential and hidden, like the wooden framework of a house, or like the unconscious—have been a focus of deconstructive theory.

Within my enquiry, I consider the narrative frames of *The Dream of the Rood*, *Daniel*, and *Beowulf*. Like all frames, those of Old English poetry guide the reader's interpretation of the text (mediate between reader and text), telling her or him that this linguistic unit exists within a larger context, yet is in some way distinct from its surroundings (so they also mediate between the general and the specific). *The Dream of the Rood* and *Daniel* are structured according to complex series of frames, with acts of interpretation encompassing passages of condensed significance. In *The Dream*, the speaking cross envelops its described experience with explanation, which, in turn, is enwrapped by the dreamer's reinterpretation and assimilation of those events, both interpretive discourses being cast in self-referential language.

Dreams, lyrics, and the miracle of the angel writing on the wall in *Daniel* are significant and surprising moments that require interpretation to link them to the narrative of the poem. In both texts, the complex process of reading is foregrounded as elaborate interpretive borders shape their narratives. Although mediation is the focus of these poems (frames are of central significance) the reader is not guided toward resolution, nor are the narratives characterized by closure. The outer frame of *Daniel*, for example, consists of the accounts of the fall of nations; here, established order collapses, walls crumble, and the narrative does not end but represents history at the threshold of repetition.

The complex narrative structure of *Beowulf* has evoked much critical attention. A number of stories—framed by a narrator's commentary, a fictional reader's response, the external audience's memory of omitted details, or the repetition of words or ideas—constitute the poem. Typically, scholars have described the stories within the story as digressions or interruptions, but there is some disagreement as to where to draw the line between such diversions and the "main" story of the poem. Two attempts have been made to visualize the narrative structure of *Beowulf*, accounting for its digressions, by creating analogies with art: Adeline Bartlett describes the poem as a tapestry and John Leyerle conceives of it as similar to the interlace designs which decorate Anglo-Saxon sculpture, jewelry, and manscripts.[17] Instead, I draw on manuscript illuminations with intricate, intriguing borders in order to address the question of what is central and what peripheral. By referring to the image of a framed picture I am focusing on the borders where the tapestry's panels meet, or the folds where the interlacing threads overlap. The decorative borders of the illuminations relate to the images they contain in ways that complicate interpretation. They do not advance the independent and finite meaning of a representation. Instead, they draw attention to themselves (so that the reader lingers in enjoyment of them and is aware of the text as something which has been crafted), and then, often, they overlap with the image, suggesting that the limit they have traced can be transgressed.

It would seem that the individually framed stories within the "main" story of *Beowulf* are, by definition, framed rather than framing elements. The internal stories collectively, though, also frame the text that contains them by providing surrounding information—telling of events which lead up to or follow from the occurrences within the story of Beowulf, or of events which are in some way parallel to them. The frame constituted of these stories is like the acanthus borders of the Benedictional of St. Æthelwold illuminations (see figs. 14 and 16). Both the narrative and the pictorial borders have a "thickness" (as Derrida says of Kant's parerga) that occupies a large proportion of the composition and also of the reader's attention; both extend into and become entangled with the "central" representation. *Beowulf*, like other Anglo-Saxon art, is elaborately structured by frames that are fluid, playful, and up to the reader's interpretation; the center and the periphery are relative and changeable.

The Opaque Text

Two models to which I continually return throughout this study are Anglo-Saxon pictorial art and Old English riddles. The contemporary manuscript illumination and sculpture are as difficult to read as the poetry; in both, the understanding of a represented story or event seems to be interrupted, rather than advanced, by the way the text is designed. Both forms are unrecuperable by conventional methods of interpretation. Since some narrative structures (such as codes of perspective and framing devices) are more easily perceived in visual art, the latter is helpful in explor-

ing relevant ways of interpreting the poetry. By considering different media, I am acknowledging that divisions between the "two" are arbitrary and
conventional; the visual and verbal texts were produced in the same culture, and taken together they reflect more about Anglo-Saxon perceptions
than either would in isolation.

The Exeter Book riddles, with their challenges "saga hwæt ic hatte"
("say what I am called") or "ræd hwæt ic mæne" ("interpret what I mean"),
explicitly entice the reader to make meaning. The kinds of questions that
they pose and their methods of guiding the reader's response reveal forms
of address present in other, less overtly enigmatic Old English poetry.
They speak of identity as problematic and constructed, of reading as the
deciphering of a puzzle, and of the written transmission of texts as intersecting in a curious way with the oral. Most generally, the riddles function
as metaphors, involving the reader in producing similarity through difference. Many of the problems that readers of Old English poetry have tended
to gloss over are conspicuously present in the riddles.

When reading practices are explored, questions of forms and locations
of mediation are at issue. As soon as the myth of a wise author conveying
his meaning through his work is discarded, the intervention that defines
interpretation becomes apparent. Catherine Belsey dates the recognition of
mediation to New Criticism's focus on the text: "The invisible thread linking two minds which defines the text in the expressive theory had become
visible, discursive, subject to 'objective' and public scrutiny."[18] The text was
recognized as having the substance of a single thread; since New Criticism,
the fabric of mediation has become at once more elaborate and less comprehensible. The text is a place of mediation, but one that is not static, not
unitary in its mode(s) of mediating, and subject itself to mediating influences, introduced through the process of reading. Structures in the text
direct our reading, but these are plural and are themselves open to interpretation.

Cultural preconceptions mediate reading and, at the same time, are
reflected in the text, most vividly through structures of mediation. Chapters 1 and 2 are concerned with locating places in the texts where reading
is being shaped and with attempting to articulate the meanings of these
interventions. The first chapter focuses on voice as a location of the text's
address to the reader. The multiplicity and ambiguity of voices in Old
English poems representing first-person speech disorient the reader. Conceptions of identity—the identity of the speaker and, by reflection, that of
the reader—ask to be reformulated. This reformulation occurs through
the questioning of the reader's place in relation to the text, and is guided
by a comparison of poetic voice to the multiple perspectives suggested by

Anglo-Saxon pictorial art. In the second chapter, mediation is explored in what is perhaps its most explicit form. Framing devices in Old English poetry—narrative divisions, repetitions of words or ideas—are, like the borders of Anglo-Saxon manuscript illuminations, so elaborate that they draw attention to themselves (mediation typically goes unnoticed), and question the very limits that they trace. My third chapter is concerned with a form of mediation specific to the transitional nature of Anglo-Saxon culture. The poetry as written in late tenth- or early eleventh-century manuscripts mediates our knowledge of the oral past, but at the same time, the past and its oral compositional structures continue to be present in the poetry's inscription and intervene in our reading of these texts.

A conception of Old English poetry as always in process, never complete and definable, underlies my thesis and is most explicitly articulated in the final chapter. This point of view follows from my concern with reading as a creative activity and also emphasizes the nonobjective status of the text. Although a view of the text as a perpetually shifting ground is a principle of postmodern theory, it has particular relevance for Old English poetry, whose performative, oral structures give the impression that it is continually being rewritten. Walter Benjamin says that in a culture that transmits its stories orally "traces of the storyteller cling to the story the way the handprints of the potter cling to the clay vessel."[19] Signs of the moment of composition—tentative framing structures, rephrasings, supplements—remain as permanent tracks of the transitory. In this study, I attempt to show how, through these still visible and audible tracks, a hermeneutics can begin to be traced.

Intersections

During much of the time I was researching and writing this book, I lamented the almost absolute lack of Old English literary scholarship that took into account the critical theoretical developments of the last several decades. Recently, though, this situation has changed significantly. Now I am able to describe my work as part of a progressive rethinking of Anglo-Saxon texts currently in process and to situate it within this framework by discussing several points of intersection between my interests and those of other scholars.

Gillian Overing, in *Language, Sign, and Gender in Beowulf*,[20] argues, as I do, that contemporary, post-Saussurean theory offers a particularly appropriate context for a rereading of *Beowulf*. She does not simply apply a specific theory to the poem as object, but responds to its semiotic struc-

tures as indicators of modes of signification. The poem can teach us about
alternative ways of reading:

> *Beowulf* . . . offers an ideal model of an already deconstructed, even a
> continually deconstructing, text. . . . Its arcane structure describes cycli-
> cal repetitions and patterned intersections of themes that baffle linear
> perspective, and suggest instead the irresolution and dynamism of the
> deconstructionist freeplay of textual elements. (p. xiii)

Overing reads *Beowulf* and works of twentieth-century theory—e.g., the
semiotics of Charles Peirce, Derrida's concept of *différance*, Hélène Cixous
and Catherine Clément's figure of woman as marginal "hysteric"—in light
of each other. Like mine, her critique stresses the "opened-endedness" of
the poem and places her subjectivity at its center. Although the texts we
have chosen to focus upon are not the same, and despite our differing
theoretical models, Overing's study and my own intersect and reinforce
each other in their redefinition of processes of signification in Anglo-Saxon
texts.

In his *Desire for Origins: New Language, Old English, and Teaching
the Tradition*,[21] Allen Frantzen is also concerned with the reception of Old
English literature. His definition of reception embraces the practices of
editing and publishing texts, as well as the activity of interpretation, and
he examines the ideological interests of Reformation, nineteenth- and
twentieth-century scholarship in Anglo-Saxon culture. The effect of Frantzen's analysis is to undermine any notion of interpretive complacency or
objectivity by locating and specifically defining interestedness. In the process of this articulation of historical prejudice, he is also demonstrating
the necessity to interpretation of subjectivity, although his stress is not on
the personal desire of the individual reader. Frantzen's critical framework
is constructed through reference to the insights of "various historians of
ideas—Michel Foucault, Hayden White, Jerome J. McGann, Edward Said,
and a number of others" (p. xv), and when he focuses on particular Anglo-
Saxon texts he chooses Bede's *Ecclesiastical History* and *Beowulf*. His
work is deconstructive with regard to the historical reception of Old English literature, rather than with regard to interpretation of the literature
itself. Nevertheless, our interests converge in their focus on the complex,
yet previously disregarded, practices of reading Anglo-Saxon texts.

Allen Frantzen has also edited a collection of articles devoted to contemporary critical methods of interpreting medieval (primarily Old English) literature. *Speaking Two Languages: Traditional Disciplines and
Contemporary Theory in Medieval Studies*[22] foregrounds interpretation as
a complex, dialogic process—"languages," in the title, refers to "critical

methods" (p. ix). The collection radically subverts conventional interpretive strategies that depend on obscuring and denying the writer's commit-
ment to, or even awareness of, any method. The theoretical frameworks of
the contributors are various—including Foucauldian, feminist, post-
Freudian, oral-formulaic, and receptionalist perspectives. All share the
premise that the interpreter's horizon of enquiry (to return to Gadamer)
necessarily exists and should be informed and articulated; this is also the
starting point of my work.

Seth Lerer describes his *Literacy and Power in Anglo-Saxon Literature*[23] as a "study of the place of texts in the construction of the Anglo-
Saxon literary imagination" (3). As I turn to selected texts as evidence of
interpretive methods, Lerer looks to a similar body of evidence in order to
locate and articulate "allegories of the making and reception of a literary
tradition" (3). His interest is in the "varieties," "implications," and "consequences" of literacy and follows from the work of such scholars as Jack
Goody, Ian Watt, Eric Havelock, Brian Stock, Charles Segal, and Franz
Baüml, who study concepts of literacy in various Western historical, ideological contexts. Our critical frames of reference overlap, as do our choices
of Anglo-Saxon narratives as evidence. Lerer, though, searches for unifying
narrative archetypes, while I seek disunity, diversity, what Overing has
called "openendedness." Attitudes toward reading—ideas about books and
interpretation—concern us both; for me, however, this interest is part of a
study of textual structures (both pictorial and poetic) and methods of interpretation.

This brief survey of recent scholarship is not meant to be comprehensive but to sketch the situation from which I write.[24] Within the complex
diversity of these rereadings of Anglo-Saxon texts and culture there is considerable common ground. Each study reveals and critiques the conventions that have dominated criticism in this field and then radically departs
from such tradition and all of its implications. Questions are raised that
disrupt previous answers. Most generally, the scholars whose work I have
described insistently place themselves within a context of contemporary
critical thought and stress the unavoidable value of subjective interpretation. I intend my "tracing of a hermeneutics of Old English poetry"
through comparison with structures visible in Anglo-Saxon art to be a
meaningful part of this ongoing, questioning dialogue.

CHAPTER 1

Locating the Reader: Perspectives in Old English Poetry and Anglo-Saxon Art

The Old English poetry that predominantly represents first-person speech implicates the reader in specific kinds of interpretive problems. Several poems depicting an individual's story of personal experience[1]—*The Wanderer, The Seafarer, Deor, The Wife's Lament, The Husband's Message, Wulf and Eadwacer*—are difficult to read either because the speakers cannot be identified or because the events of their narratives do not form coherent, logical patterns. The Old English riddles play with precisely these questions of determining a speaker's identity and making sense of the details of "its" narrative. Although *The Dream of the Rood* does not as obviously present these kinds of interpretive problems, it too begins with a description of a mysterious, unnamed object, which only gradually identifies itself through speaking its history.

It is not coincidental that poems representing first-person speech are the most difficult Old English poems for a present-day reader to interpret. The project of that reader includes, as one of its activities, identifying (with) the characters and events portrayed in a narrative in order to make the world of the text comprehensible. This process can be described spatially: the reader sees clearly defined characters within the context of their stories and finds a position in relation to the representation. If the project of the tenth-century reader were different from reading practices with which we are more familiar, characters and their locations would be represented differently, with the result that the tracing of a reader's perspective would be problematic. In poems focusing on the experience and identity of a character, these obstacles would be especially difficult. To imagine the identification of (and with) characters in spatial terms is to suggest an analogy between poetic and pictorial depiction of narrative. Perspective in Anglo-Saxon manuscript illumination and sculpture is as difficult to "read" as the poetic portrayal of characters; since it is more easily visualized, perspective in graphic art will guide my interpretation of the reader's position in relation to Old English poetry.

Both the Old English poem *The Wanderer* and the illustrations of Genesis in MS Junius 11 (Oxford, Bodleian Library)[2] present the reader with the problem of discovering her or his position in relation to the text. Characters, actions, and scenes are described from a number of vantage points, and no authoritative voice (in the case of the poem) or pictorial code (for the drawings) explains their relationship or chronology. Reading *The Wanderer* involves, first of all, questioning the identity of the speaker(s). By identifying with a narrator or a character, the reader would be able to define a stable position from which to comprehend the text; she or he could "see" the events described from that person's point of view. The narrative voices in *The Wanderer*, though, complicate, rather than guide, the reading process. Shifts between first-person and third-person narration, changes in the tone of the speech, and two "swa cwæð" ("so spoke") clauses with ambiguous reference hinder our designation of the source of the speech and cause disorientation. Interpretations of the poem have depended upon the definition of speech boundaries (the limits of each "character's" speech), and following from this, the description of unified, believable characters; as many definitions and descriptions have been suggested as there are commentators.

The problem with this approach is that it does not allow for the possibility of letting the complications and ambiguities stand and of reading in a different way, from a shifting perspective.[3] The Junius drawings call for such a method of reading. Characters in these illustrations are not depicted consistently (details of their description may change from scene to scene, or the same character may be represented twice in a single illustration), events are not arranged sequentially (several scenes are often included on one page, with no indication of their chronology), and space is fragmented so that no one viewing position is possible. The images do not define for the reader a place from which to watch the events unfold. In this chapter, the Junius drawings will serve as a model for a reading of *The Wanderer*, which considers the meanings of the poem's multiple voices and perspectives. I shall also draw on recent theories of cinematic representation that address questions similar to those posed by *The Wanderer* and the Junius drawings—questions of perspective, subject position, and identification.

MS Junius 11: Illustrations of a Shifting Perspective

While reference to "place" is metaphoric in a discussion of the relationship of reader to poetic text, it takes on a more literal meaning in the description of the reading of a painting. In the process of interpretation the viewer, guided by codes of perspective, takes up an imaginary position in relation to the depicted scene. In order to understand the problems of perspective in the Junius drawings, I shall describe some visual codes that situate the viewer in a stable position. Renaissance perspective, a way of painting and seeing formulated in fifteenth-century Italy and dominant still, describes for the viewer a vantage point that corresponds to the former position of the painter.[4] The viewer sees as the painter saw, and an identification between the two is established. In *Vision and Painting: The Logic of the Gaze*, Norman Bryson summarizes and interprets Alberti's statement of this principle (*De Pictura*, ca. 1435):

> The eye of the viewer is to take up a position in relation to the scene that is identical to the position originally occupied by the painter, as though both painter and viewer looked through the same viewfinder onto a world unified spatially around the centric ray, the line running from viewpoint to vanishing point . . . unified spatially but also informationally, since all data represented by the image are to cohere around a core narrative structure.[5]

For the viewer of a painting to align her or his gaze with that of the painter is similar to the reader of a literary text identifying with the narrator; both processes involve screening out different possible ways of seeing, and understanding, the represented event, so that only one (limited) view is available. In doing so, the viewer or reader becomes riveted in a fixed location.

Roland Barthes describes Renaissance perspective as one manifestation of a relationship between geometry and theatre that determines the position of the subject:

> The stage is the line which stands across the path of the optic pencil, tracing at once the point at which it is brought to a stop and, as it were, the threshold of its ramification. . . . [T]here will . . . be representation for so long as a subject (author, reader, spectator or voyeur) casts his gaze towards a horizon on which he cuts out the base of a triangle, his eye (or his mind) forming the apex.[6]

The subject is locked into her or his position at the apex; this structure has prevailed in and defined predominant forms of representation in Western cultures.

Cinema inherited a system of depiction dependent on codes of Renaissance perspective with all of their implications: the camera substitutes for the painter, the spectator's view is aligned with that of the camera, and camera movement is restricted to reinforce the stationary position of the viewer. Because of the camera's potential for many kinds of movement, such constraints are significant; the camera serves to contain the spectator's "look." This theory of cinematic representation was first developed by Christian Metz and is central to Stephen Heath's work on narrative, framing, and other systems of "suture" in cinema.[7] Heath reviews the problem in "Lessons from Brecht":

> [F]rom the perfecting of the camera itself as instrument to the elaboration and codification of the rules of film making and construction . . . it is this coherence of the subject-eye in its relation to the image that is crucial . . . the camera . . . is 'perfected' towards . . . the placing of the subject in a fixed relation to a stable 'Reality'. . . . Everything in the mainstream (commercial) development of the camera, movie camera, editing and continuity techniques and so on is then fashioned to this position.[8]

The reader of a painting executed according to the rules of Renaissance perspective and the reader of a conventional narrative film are held in position and presented with coherent, easily comprehended images.

This way of reading images, which has prevailed for five centuries, is only one method of seeing; there were and are others. It would be anachronistic to speak of the eleventh-century drawings of the Junius manuscript as deviating from Renaissance codes; rather, they represent another way of seeing. The depiction of space in the Junius drawings does not indicate a position in which a painter once stood.[9] The reader is not directed by the image to align her or his view with that of the artist and to see in a particular way. Pages 11, 13, and 73 of the manuscript (figs. 1, 2, and 3) split the view of the reader so that she or he is at once above and in front of the subject matter; the viewer looks down on heaven (fig. 1) and the sea (fig. 2), while looking from a position somewhere in front of the images at the scenes of paradise, and in one illustration of the ark (fig. 3) one of its sides and the deck are seen simultaneously. Several of the illustrations (ms. p 9, fig. 4) depict more than one scene within a single frame, each scene having its own groundline; the reader cannot assume any single position in relation to this geography.

The (imagined) physical place of the viewer is at issue in a discussion of reading pictorial representation; questions of time, sequence, and narrative follow from a tracing of the reader's position(s). If Renaissance perspective implies a single viewing position and a stationary viewer, it also restricts that viewer to seeing a particular narrative moment. The illustration of God bending over Adam as he sleeps, touching Eve's hand and blessing her, and of the angels moving between heaven and paradise (fig. 4) depicts several time periods that are not arranged sequentially. The viewer's perception of time parallels her or his perception of space; neither a physical nor a temporal perspective is defined by the painting. The two

1. God in heaven, Adam and Eve in paradise. Oxford Bodleian MS Junius 11, p. 11.

figures of God in this drawing do not present a problem of interpretation since they each belong to a different scene. In the illustration of the sentencing of Adam and Eve (ms. p 44, fig. 5), however, the double figure of God is more difficult to understand. If the reader introduces narrative sequence to the image—God sentenced Eve and then Adam—the repetition becomes comprehensible. The drawing itself, though, represents two time periods simultaneously and does not direct the reader's interpretation of them.

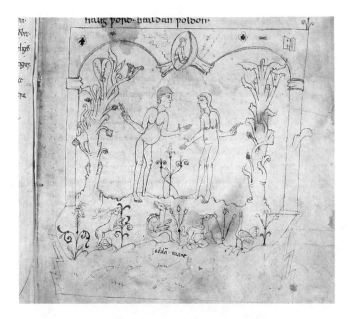

2. Adam and Eve in paradise. Oxford Bodleian MS Junius 11, p. 13.

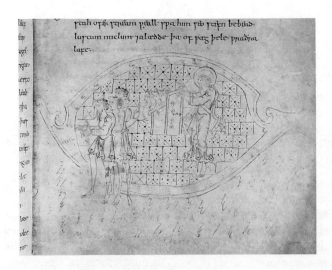

3. Noah and family leaving ark. Oxford Bodleian MS Junius 11, p. 73.

4. God putting Adam to sleep and creating Eve. Angels in heaven.
Oxford Bodleian MS Junius 11, p. 9.

Narrative sequence must be brought to the drawings by the reader if the multiple scenes and repetition of characters are to be understood. No consistent reading pattern is indicated by the arrangement of the scenes on a manuscript page. Following the order of the narrative, a page can be read diagonally (from lower right to upper left, fig. 4), from left to right (fig. 5), from bottom to top (fig. 6), from top to bottom (fig. 7), or in any of several other directions. Knowledge of the story (provided by the reader), not the systematic depiction of the order of events (found in the text), shapes the reading process. Sightlines do sometimes guide the reader from scene to scene.[10] In figure 6, the eye is led from the strong

5. Sentencing of Adam and Eve. Oxford Bodleian MS Junius 11, p. 44.

6. Satan sending messenger who tempts Eve. Oxford Bodleian MS Junius 11, p. 20.

scolde he þabnadanligar · sécan helle gehlið·
þæn hir hcinna læz · —

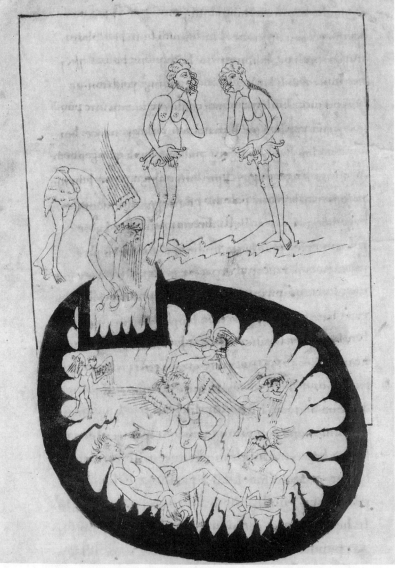

7. The messenger returning to Satan. Oxford Bodleian MS Junius 11, p. 36.

diagonal line of Satan's body, following his gaze, to the messenger's departure through the gate of hell, and then to the tree and the serpent directly above him. The look exchanged between the serpent and Eve forms the next visual link, and Eve's gesture toward herself and Adam beside the forbidden tree completes the story. As in the illustration of the sentencing of Adam and Eve (fig. 5), a character is represented twice in what appears to be one scene. By following the sightlines and by knowing the story, the reader can interpret the depiction of Adam and Eve as representing the "direct speech" of Eve: she tells the serpent of God's previous interdiction.

Often, though, sightlines reinforce the separateness of the scenes. In figure 4, the taking of Adam's rib is not indicated as leading to the creation of Eve; God bends over Adam, the curve of his back bracketing this scene from the rest of the page. The exchanged look of God and Eve, and the diagonal movement of the angel toward a framed heaven, mark these scenes as being separate elements. The illustrations of the Junius manuscript are episodic. Gaps between narrative moments—unstated temporal relationships and other missing explanatory links—must be filled by the reader's memory of a story she or he already knows.[11] I have proposed a correspondence between reading from a shifting perspective and active reading, where the reader participates in the meaning of the text; the reader's role in the construction of the narrative illustrated in MS Junius 11 is an instance of this process.

The Wanderer: Questions of Voice and Identity

The Junius drawings do not describe for the viewer a precise physical (or temporal) position; instead, they allow her or him to see from many perspectives. The difficulties of reading The Wanderer, which are not so easily visualized, can be understood in light of this interpretive practice. Just as there is no one viewing position for the reader of the Junius drawings, there is no single narrative point of view available to the reader of The Wanderer. The problems begin with the interpretation of two "swa cwæð" clauses:

Swa cwæð eardstapa,   earfeþa gemyndig,
wraþra wælsleahta,   winemæga hryre: (6–7)

Swa cwæð snottor on mode,   gesæt him sundor æt rune.   (111)[12]

These lines may refer back to what has just been said, forward to the speech that follows, or both. Whether the "eardstapa" (line 6) and the "snottor" (111) are to be understood as the same person depends upon the interpretation of "swa cwæð"; it is possible that the lines which are enclosed by these two passages, and which make up most of the poem, represent the speech of a single person. Lines 8–110, however, cannot easily be read as one unified speech; they include several changes of tone, and the speaker sometimes relates his own experiences and sometimes those of a third person. The tone of several statements attributed to the "eardstapa" / "snottor" resembles that of lines 1–5 and 112–15, passages usually placed outside quotation marks by editors; perhaps the speaker of lines 8–110, who makes generalizations and utters precepts, is also the speaker of the homiletic opening and closing lines.

If the interpretation of "swa cwæð" were the only problem in identifying the speaker(s) of *The Wanderer*, an Anglo-Saxon audience may not have found identification difficult. In the process of oral delivery, a performer would probably have used gesture and intonation to make the referents more clearly understood. Ambiguity deriving from the shifts in "a" speaker's manner of addressing the reader, and from shifts in "his" mood, complicates interpretation for any reader. Recently, critics have used our present-day problem with the interpretation of "swa cwæð" as a starting point in their attempts to resolve the poem's ambiguities by defining firm speech boundaries. Many such attempts have been made. Bernard F. Huppé's suggestion that *The Wanderer* comprises two monologues, one delivered by a wanderer and the other by a wiseman,[13] is contested by Stanley Greenfield, who argues that lines 8–110 "are best taken as one speech uttered by an 'eardstapa' who has with the passage of time become a 'snottor.'"[14] John C. Pope at first read *The Wanderer* as a dialogue: the "eardstapa" begins the colloquy by describing his personal troubles—the loss of his lord, his solitude—and speaking of others with similar misfortunes (1–5, 8–57), then the "snottor on mode" who is wiser and more philosophical in his outlook, goes on to lament death and destruction throughout the world (58–110). Although Pope later retracted this interpretation and defined *The Wanderer* as being a monologue, he still saw a clear distinction between the nature of the speech early in the poem and that after line 58; the speaker develops throughout the poem, broadening his concerns and gaining wisdom.[15]

T. P. Dunning and A. J. Bliss come to much the same conclusion as Pope; the poem is a "dramatic monologue" depicting the maturing process of the wanderer who undergoes a major "transition" at line 58.[16] The Christian sentiments expressed in lines 1–5 and 112–15 are seen by Ida Masters Hollowell to distinguish those passages from the rest of the poem. She attributes lines 8–110 to a "woðbora"—a pagan seer—comparing him to the poet in *The Order of the World*; like Pope, Dunning, and Bliss, she not only defines speech boundaries but describes a personality for the speaker.[17] Rosemary Woolf does not do this; she sees lines 8–110 as being unified and coherent by virtue of their identity as a "planctus," rather than because they originate with a psychologically described character. While she lets the ambiguities of the speech stand, she nevertheless places the reader by asking her or him to read the poem according to its similarities with other poetry of a particular genre.[18]

Instead of attributing the voices in *The Wanderer* to a specific character (or characters), whose personality could then be elaborated, I shall begin by describing the different kinds of speech that constitute the poem; these are tentative definitions since I shall go on to show that even here there are no firm boundaries, but one type blends into another.[19] Most prevalent is a voice that makes descriptive statements about typical characters[20] and, on one occasion, about the fallen state of the world (lines 75–87). It always maintains some degree of distance from the object of its description (although the degree varies), it never explicitly identifies itself, and there is usually no voice beyond it, which could limit or contextualize its statements.[21] This is a voice of experience and wisdom which cannot easily be questioned. The "swa cwæð" passages are instances of a second kind of speech, also without a stated source, but distinct from the first in that it should function to bridge sections of the narrative and create frames for discrete passages of direct speech; such informative statements should provide structure and guide the reader. In *The Wanderer*, though, the referents of the "swa cwæð" clauses are not clear, and they add little to the coherence of the poem. Identifiable voices, placed within a context, make up the remainder of the speech in *The Wanderer*. Lines 8–11a, 19–29a, and 58–62a are in the first person.

> Oft ic sceolde ana   uhtna gehwylce
> mine ceare cwiþan.   Nis nu cwicra nan
> þe ic him modsefan   minne durre
> sweotule asecgan.   (8–11a)[22]

> [S]wa ic modsefan   minne sceolde,
> oft earmcearig,   eðle bidæled,
> freomægum feor   feterum sælan,
> siþþan geara iu   goldwinne minne
> hrusan heolstre biwrah,   ond ic hean þonan
> wod wintercearig   ofer waþema gebind,
> sohte sele dreorig   sinces bryttan,
> hwær ic feor oþþe neah   findan meahte
> þone þe in meaduhealle   min mine wisse,

oþþe mec freondleasne   frefran wolde,
weman mid wynnum.   (19–29a)[23]

Forþon ic geþencan ne mæg   geond þas woruld
for hwan modsefa   min ne gesweorce,
þonne ic eorla lif   eal geondþence,
hu hi færlice   flet ofgeafon,
modge maguþegnas.   (58–62a)[24]

This kind of speech is represented as having a specified character as its source, a person who serves, within the fiction of the narrative, as a real-life example of the situation being described. A character who speaks is portrayed as being an individual like the individual reader, and when this character says "I," she or he implies the presence of the one being addressed, the reader ("you"). The reader can then take a position in relation to the speaker; a listener's role has been defined. Lines 92–110 are also direct speech, but the speaker of this passage, the man wise in spirit ["frod in ferðe," 90a], does not explicitly refer to himself by saying "I." He does state the immediacy of his speech when he says "Now the wall stands . . ." (97–8) and in his repetition of "here is" (four times in 109–10). Such adverbs of time and place refer back to the deliverer of the speech, and situate his statement[25]; the first passage of direct, first-person discourse in the poem is also fixed in the present by the adverb "nu" (9). The objective voice in *The Wanderer*, which makes descriptive statements, speaks of past, future, and of distant places but not of here and now.[26]

The one exception to this classification of the use of adverbs is at line 75 when a speaker not identified as "I" begins to describe the fallen state of the world: "swa nu missenlice / geond þisne middangeard . . ." ("so now in various places throughout this world"). In the passage immediately preceding, a wise man has been introduced, his qualities described, and he has been said to understand "hu gæstlic bið / þonne ealre þisse worulde wela weste stondeð" (73b–74; "how ghostly it will be when all the wealth of this world stands waste"). From a statement delivered by an unnamed speaker about a distant time, we are jolted into the present and compelled to ask who is making this comparison between a future state and the (fictional) present condition of the world. Two kinds of speech overlap here—the voice situated in the present enters unannounced into a speech by the voice free of context—so that the reader does not know by whom she or he is being addressed.

There are many places in the poem where such a merging of voices occurs. Since first-person discourse can potentially strengthen the identification of the reader with a fictional character (and thereby with the text),

the confusion of this type of speech with another causes the greatest disorientation. The shift from the "eardstapa's" description of his own sor-
rows and solitude (8–11, quoted above) to his comments on the prudent
speech of a nobleman (11b–18) is not easily comprehended.

> Ic to soþe wat
> þæt biþ in eorle   indryhten þeaw,
> þæt he his ferðlocan   fæste binde,
> healde his hordcofan,   hycge swa he wille.
> Ne mæg werig mod   wyrde wiðstondan,
> ne se hreo hyge   helpe gefremman.
> Forðon domgeorne   dreorigne oft
> in hyra breostcofan   bindað fæste;   (11b–18)[27]

Although these lines are among the passages I have defined as being objective in tone, they are given a context by the speaker's introduction, "Ic to
soþe wat þæt" ("I know truly that"). This passage has the effect of being
first-person and third-person speech simultaneously: it is designated as the
speech of the "eardstapa," but it sounds like other passages in the poem that
are not attributed to a specific person and that also describe the behavior of a
typical character. In particular, the resemblance in tone between lines 11b–
18 and lines 1–5 causes difficulty since the introductory passage—objective,
detached, and free of context—has just been read.

> Oft him anhaga   are gebideð,
> metudes miltse,   þeah þe he modcearig
> geond lagulade   longe sceolde
> hreran mid hondum   hrimcealde sæ,
> wadan wræclastas.   Wyrd bið ful aræd!   (1–5)[28]

The identity of "I" in *The Wanderer* is drawn into question: what distin-
guishes his voice and where are its limits?

When the first-person speaker introduces a "fictional" third person
whose experiences closely resemble his own, he divides his identity in two.
After lamenting the loss of his lord and his solitary wanderings (19–29a,
quoted above), the "eardstapa" invites the sympathy of the reader: "Wat se
þe cunnað, / hu sliþen bið sorg to gefaran, / þam þe him lyt hafað leofra
geholena" (29b–31; "The one who experiences knows how cruel sorrow is
as a companion for the one who has few dear protectors"). The reader—
the implied second person—is directed away from an immediate identification with the first-person narrator and asked to relate to the experience
of a hypothetical third person. Within the fiction of the poem the "eard-

stapa" ("I") knows the inner thoughts of this third person ("Þinceð him on mode" [41a; "It seems to him in his mind"], "maga gemynd mod geondhweorfeð" [51; "his mind wanders through the memory of kinsmen"), and the third person understands the "eardstapa's" sufferings. The limits of the identities of these "two" people are not defined, and the reader is never secure in a position relative to that of the speaker. The situation becomes even more confused with the introduction of the wise man ("forþon ne mæg weorþan wis wer, ær he age / wintra dæl in woruldrice" [64–65a]; "therefore a man may not become wise before he has a share of winters in the world"); this character also shares the identity of the first-person speaker, "both" having similar visions of the world in ruins. Throughout the poem, the reader is continually shifting between closeness to the character who relates his experiences directly and distance from the (same) character described as "the one who."

The representation of place in *The Wanderer* does not help the reader to become situated. Since the first-person speaker does not locate himself in any particular setting, the reader, unable to imagine the described scenes in relation to a constant, primary location, witnesses them as a series of tableaux.[29] Several vivid scenes are presented as occurring through the eyes, or in the minds, of the poem's "various characters." After telling of the sadness of "one who has few dear protectors," the speaker describes that person's mental images:

> Þinceð him on mode   þæt he his mondryhten
> clyppe ond cysse,   ond on cneo lecge
> honda ond heafod,   swa he hwilum ær
> in geardagum   giefstolas breac.   (41–44)[30]

The reader, in picturing the scene of a retainer kneeling before a throne and worshipping his lord, shares—by way of the voice of the "eardstapa"—the exile's dream of the past. Upon wakening, this joyless man sees before him:

>   fealwe wegas,
> baþian brimfuglas,   brædan feþra,
> hreosan hrim ond snaw,   hagle gemenged.   (46b–48)[31]

Again the reader experiences the perceptions of the exile as mediated through the first-person speaker's description; the bleak vision represents the exile's present reality. Dream and reality become confused in the next scene, as his mind wanders through the memory of kinsmen:

greteð gliwstafum,   georne geondsceawað
secga geseldan.   Swimmað eft on weg!
Fleotendra ferð   no þær fela bringeð
cuðra cwidegiedda.   (52–55a)[32]

To read this passage is to participate in the exile's confusion; the reader
must try to picture a situation for this scene, to imagine who is swimming
away—the birds or the companions, and to conceive of a "spirit of floating
ones."

Two desolate landscapes are depicted in *The Wanderer*. The first is not
designated as being the vision of any particular character, yet (as discussed
above) it occurs within the poem's present:

                                        geond þisne middangeard
winde biwaune   weallas stondaþ,
hrime bihrorene,   hryðge þa ederas.
Woriað þa winsalo,   waldend licgað
dreame bidrorene,   duguþ eal gecrong,
wlonc bi wealle.   (75b–80a)[33]

This landscape is difficult to comprehend since it is not assigned a place in
the poem; neither through narrative logic nor through linking the vision
to the consciousness of a character does the poem tell the reader how to
understand the image. The man "wise in spirit" also sees his world in
ruins:

Stondeð nu on laste   leofre duguþe
weal wundrum heah,   wyrmlicum fah.
Eorlas fornoman   asca þryþe,
wæpen wælgifru,   wyrd seo mære,
ond þas stanhleoþu   stormas cnyssað,
hrið hreosende   hrusan bindeð,
wintres woma,   þonne won cymeð,
nipeð nihtscua,   norþan onsendeð
hreo hæglfare   hæleþum on andan.   (97–105)[34]

In its images of death, storms, and the vestiges of a culture, this scene
greatly resembles the previous vision of decay. According to the poem's
representation of speakers, though, the second scene is described by a
different person; the reader now shares the perspective of the wise man,
who addresses the audience directly through first-person speech.

Reading *The Wanderer* involves imagining a sequence of tableaux, some of which are "real," some fantastic. The voice of the "eardstapa" seems to guide the reader through these landscapes, but since his relationship to the "other" characters (who sometimes are represented as the source of the visions) is ambiguous, the reader does not see the landscapes from a defined perspective. She or he has limited vision, only being able to see what is immediately present to the eyes or the mind of a particular character. The reader of *The Wanderer* is "too close" to the characters who describe their visions; the poem offers no vantage point far enough away from the scenes to allow a wider, more inclusive, view.[35] Like the reader of the Junius drawings, this reader must provide the narrative links, binding the separate scenes to each other and to the rest of the poem. The temporal relationships between the scenes in *The Wanderer* seem to be signaled by adverbs, but these do not always fix the scene in a context; the "nu" of the second vision of desolation refers to the time of the wise man's speech, which itself is not clearly placed in relation to the rest of the poem. Since the first such vision also describes a present state, these two images may overlap in tense as well as subject matter, but this is not certain. As discussed above, the first description of the world's fallen state is preceded by the lines: "Ongietan sceal gleaw hæle hu gæstlic bið, / þonne ealre þisse worulde wela weste stondeð, / swa nu missenlice geond þisne middangeard . . ." (73–75; "A wise man must understand how ghostly it will be when all the wealth of this world stands waste, just as now in various places throughout the world . . ."). If "bið" is translated as "will be" and the "gleaw hæle" is assumed to be the man "frod in ferðe" (90; i.e., the wise man through whose eyes we see the second image of desolation), this second vision would occur in the future. *The Wanderer* reflects the Junius drawings' unspecified time frame—neither text directs the reader's interpretation of temporal relationships between depicted scenes.

First-person discourse implies the presence of a second person; the reader assumes the role of "you" in relation to the speaker's "I" and an identification between the two is established. Although this form of address suggests a close relationship between the reader and the character, according to *The Wanderer*'s representation of place the reader "stands beside" not the first-person speaker but a third person—either an exile or a wise man.[36] The descriptions of place in the poem can be understood as subjective, yet they call into question the very notion of subjectivity. While the voice we hear directly is that of the "eardstapa," we see through the eyes of other characters; in *The Wanderer* voice and vision are split, emanating from different sources. The first-person speaker does not have a distinct identity but rather one that merges with those of the exile and the wise man; his voice does not represent a unified and unique consciousness. The poem's scattered scenes reflect the speaker's multifaceted identity, and the reader can neither focus upon a central character nor find a position in relation to a coherent geography. Readers of *The Wanderer* (like those of the Junius drawings) are unable to place themselves, to imagine themselves as being still.

I would like to propose that the unexpected redirection of the speaker's and the reader's focus—away from the "eardstapa" and toward the "other" characters and their visions—indicates and results from a particular orientation of identity. Rather than turning inward in his suffering, the wanderer is depicted as sharing his experience with (other) fictional characters and with the audience/reader. The wanderer is not represented as a self-contained individual, isolated within his inexpressible, unshareable sorrow. His response to sadness and isolation contrasts with that depicted in Romantic and post-Romantic literature; vestiges of this literature's construction of individualism remain in our present modes of signification and interpretation. In Romantic poetry, individual poets are represented as the source of their experience, emotion, and art. They often speak in the first person of isolation from society, but this is an inevitable solitude, an "inviolate retirement" (Wordsworth, *Recluse*). The Romantic poets' detachment from others is not only a physical one; they frequently represent themselves as lingering within subjective mental states. In contrast, the exiled wanderer is depicted as a speaker who describes the merging of his experience, thoughts, and identity with those of others. Through his speech, the wanderer recreates a community—this time a community of understanding—to replace the one he has lost; through this process he identifies himself.

The Wanderer is a product of a community-oriented culture. In Anglo-Saxon England, a person's position within the structure of a community—formed by bonds either to kin or to a lord—placed her or him within a network of rights and duties.[37] A place in the community provided one with a social identity; the individual was recognized if her or his family or lord was known. Recognition and identification came through others, through the community that surrounded and contained the individual. The importance of kindred and lord is explicit in the story of *The Wanderer* and has already been much discussed; what has been neglected is the way the significance of community may shape conceptions of self, and the way such ideas of self and community may in turn have an effect on the telling of a story.

The community did not only provide individuals with credentials, it also took responsibility for their actions.[38] This obligation for the personal marks an intersection of the community's role in the individual's social identity and its role in the shaping of her or his self identity; at the same time as the community's responsibility functions to provide the individual with a social place, it also says that one's own actions—what one "chooses" to do and then carries out—are ultimately in the domain of responsibility of others. A different conception of self—unlike present-day ideas of individualism and self-sufficiency—is suggested by such a merging of the territories of self and others. Perhaps borders between the "two" realms were defined differently, or not defined at all.

The wanderer's process of identifying himself through others is represented as occurring around the very question of speaking. He knows that a nobleman should be prudent of speech (11b–13), and that those eager for glory should bind their sadness in their heart (17–18), so he himself should do the same (19–21). This is a moment of transition for the speaker as he moves, in mid sentence, from uttering precepts to describing personal experience:

> swa ic modsefan   minne sceolde,
> oft earmcearig,   eðle bidæled,
> freomægum feor   feterum sælan,
> siþþan geara iu   goldwine minne
> hrusan heolstre biwrah . . .   (19–23a)[39]

Adjectival phrases describing the personal situation of the subject ("ic") fall within the speaker's statement of proper behavior, and introduce the story of his past. "I" as someone who should act in the same way as others who are "domgeorne," and "I" as someone with a particular history are both the grammatical subjects of the same sentence. The identification of the speaker with those eager for glory is presented as the impulse for the change of tone, the point at which his knowledge of proper codes of behavior and his memory of experience merge; the path leading to the wanderer's thoughts about himself passes first through his knowledge of the customs and behavior of others.

Representation—the process of telling a story—is caught up in a web of (concepts of) identity and social structure; it at once derives from these concepts, speaks of them, and reproduces them. Wherever questions about *The Wanderer* begin, they move on to ask about the related issues. The receiver of the text—the audience or reader—is not excluded from the design of representation; examining the place of the present-day reader and of the reader in the tenth or eleventh century is one way to begin questioning the text. If the difficulties of identification posed by *The Wanderer* are accepted (both the identification of the speaker[s] and the reader's identification with the text), questions arise concerning self-conception, the role of community, and the nature of the reading process.

By locating the present-day reader in relation, first, to a conventional, contemporary text (a novel or a film) and then to *The Wanderer*, I shall begin to sketch a situation for the poem's Anglo-Saxon audience. The setting for the twentieth-century reading process, described in its simplest, most physical terms, is one of a reader's private interaction with a text. As she or he sits alone, the reader is caught up in a direct identification with the text—her or his mirror image; the wholeness and completeness desired by the reader is reflected and guaranteed by that of the represented characters.[40] In order that this structure be sustained, the characters must display individuality and psychological unity; at risk is the disorientation and fragmentation of the reader. The direct relationship of individual reader to text, fundamental to the modern reading process, carries over into other modes of representation. In cinema, although there is a group audience, the individual viewer is addressed, held in place, and "shown" her or his identity by the conventions of filmic depiction. Mary Ann Doane's work on voice, space, and identity in cinema addresses issues related to those central to the problem of locating the reader of *The Wanderer*.[41] The voice, in classical narrative film, belongs to the individual; when it is "anchored in a given body," it functions to "lend to the character the consistency of the real" (36). In order to create an "aural illusion of position" (45), the voice must emanate from the screen where the visual "spectacle" is "unfolding" (38). The voice, in supporting the representation of a unified character, places the spectator in relation to the film's fiction and "[holds] at bay the potential trauma of dispersal, dismemberment, difference" (45).

Sound in cinema, though, has always been a possible source of disruption; in order for the voice to seem the property of an individual, careful work has gone into binding it to an image. In some postmodern cinema, potential combinations of voice and image are explored, and the unity of the fictional subject is fractured.[42] This prevents the viewer from assuming a passive, stationary position, held in place by her or his identification with that subject. Present-day readers of *The Wanderer*, unable to identify (with) the poem's speaker(s), find themselves similarly disoriented as they face a split between voice and vision. Returning to the image of the text as a mirror (the film screen is particularly conducive to this metaphor),[43] the reader of *The Wanderer*, like the viewer of such cinema can be understood to receive a multifaceted reflection that can only be resolved if she or he moves and sees from a variety of perspectives.

The similarity between *The Wanderer* and a postmodern text may be attributable to their resistance to what I have described as a conventional reading process; structures of identity which the experimental film subverts—those based on a direct and private relationship of reader and text—would not have been firmly in place in tenth- or eleventh-century

England.[44] Although *The Wanderer* is a written text (suggesting the possibility of private reading), it retains vestiges of its oral history; alliteration,
formulaic units, and variation are structures that speak of the process of
composition, the poem's ongoing formulation in the presence of an audience.[45] Despite its inscription, *The Wanderer* would probably have been
read aloud to an audience. Although as early as the late ninth century
Alfred suggested that young people of England who had the means
("speda" has been interpreted both as "wealth" and as "capability") be educated "until the time when they can read English writing well," Ælfric,
who wrote between the years 989 and ca. 1010 (his writings are roughly
contemporary with the Exeter Book), dedicated his first collection of homilies to an audience of both readers and listeners. Throughout his homilies
and saints' lives, he addresses "se ðe þæt ræde, oþþe rædan gehyre." These
texts were probably written for an uneducated lay audience and meant to
be read publicly, by a priest. By the late tenth century, oral culture was
still prevalent. Whether the Exeter manuscript would have been read privately or publicly depends upon whom we consider to have made up its
audience.[46]

The fiction of the poem describes an immediate, oral relating of thought
and experience. Inscribed in a manuscript, *The Wanderer* traces for itself—in
what it represents and in its mode of representation—a situation of oral
delivery. Just as the physical setting for reading a contemporary novel indicates and perpetuates a psychological process of identification, the locale for
oral reading has a particular significance. When there is a collective audience, the personal and private relation of reader to text is lost. A group is
addressed rather than an individual; therefore, what has been seen as fundamental to the silent reading of a modern text is absent, and a distinct
process of identification can occur. The audience member—one of a
group—would look to the text with no expectation of seeing her or his
individuality reflected. The representation of characters would not have to
be structured to protect any image of the reader's own self-containment;
in *The Wanderer*, speech boundaries and, following from this, speakers' per-
sonalities could be undefined. The heterogeneity masked by the conventional,
twentieth-century text (to guard against the reader's disorientation) faces the
composite audience of the orally delivered poem.[47]

When a text was spoken to a group, bonds of community were recon-
firmed, not the uniqueness of the individual reader. At this social gathering the listener would take her or his place among others. Not just the
setting, though, bound the individual listener to the group; the text also
worked to create a community.[48] Much Old English poetry is allusive; *Beowulf* and *Deor*, in particular, refer to several stories told only in part.
Through their intertextuality, the poems would have called upon the audi-

ence's shared memory of a narrative. The listener, in order to complete the story, provided knowledge already held by her- or himself and the other members of the audience.[49] Through this process, members of the audience interacted with the text, the storyteller, and the other listeners. The drawings of the Junius manuscript are similar to such poetry in their narrative structure. Although the book would be looked at by only one reader at a time (so that reading the illustrations would not draw together members of a group), that reader would actively participate in shaping the narrative, filling in the gaps of a story that was only partially represented. While the poem was being spoken, it was becoming inscribed in the memory of each audience member and their collection of shared memories was increasing.[50] If *The Wanderer* were delivered orally, storytelling would occur at two levels; the story told by the fictional speaker(s) represented in the poem would at the same time be told by a performer to a listening audience. This audience would be implicated in both tellings. When the wanderer (the fictional speaker) says "he who has experienced knows . . . ," he is reenacting the storyteller's role of including the audience in the story; both speakers are referring to a shared (memory of) experience and thereby creating a community of listeners who gather around them and their narrative.[51]

If the tenth-century reader of *The Wanderer* were part of a listening audience, there would be an incongruity, throughout the delivery of the poem, between the fact of the performer's speaking and the meaning of what he said.[52] The listener would tentatively misidentify the voice of the performer as being one with the fictional voices that say "swa cwæð" and that make general descriptive statements. These voices are not represented as having a specific source, so they could easily be assigned to the performer. The incongruity here is between the detached, objective tone of this type of speech—like the voice-over in cinema, it could be described as "disembodied"—and the physical presence of the performer. The voice in the poem that describes typical characters never speaks of here and now, but the performer exists in the present. The act of his speaking in a public situation would contradict the statements of the first-person speaker in a very apparent way. When the "eardstapa" begins to speak he describes himself as being alone: "Nis nu cwicra nan / þe ic him modsefan minne durre / sweotule asecgan" (9b–11; "Now there is no one alive to whom I dare speak my heart openly"). Like those who are eager for praise, he must seal his heart: "[I]c modsefan minne sceolde, / . . . feterum sælan" (19–21; "I have had to seal my heart with fetters"). When the performer speaks of "his" solitude and silence, his words are manifestly untrue of his present situation.[53] Oral delivery would seem to unite two time periods so that the "here and now" of the text becomes one with that of the audience, yet there would always be a discrepancy between the described and the experienced situations: the silent, lonely wanderer speaks in a crowd, in the midst of universal desolation that does not exist. The reader would be in a position of both believing and not believing. A performed text would not seem as immediate (unmediated) as one read privately; the audience, although close to the performer, would be distanced from the poem, never submerged in its fiction.

It is difficult to locate the reader of *The Wanderer* because the text reflects a different way of reading, which occurs within a particular cultural environment and is supported by and supports specific conceptions of identity. The difference does not exist only at the level of expression. The wanderer identifies himself through the telling of his story, which is also the recreating of a community; he becomes part of a society of listeners/readers and those who have suffered just as he has. The reader watches and is drawn into this process but not from a single vantage point.[54] Only a text that represents distinct characters, who are placed in relation to each other according to a clear code of perspective, can produce—as its reflection—a stationary, self-contained reader. The speaker(s) of *The Wanderer* cannot be identified according to an interpretive practice suited to conventional novels and mainstream cinema. The Junius drawings, similarly, must be read in a particular way that is unlike the way we would read pictures drawn according to, for example, Renaissance perspective. Neither the representation of speech in *The Wanderer* nor the depiction of narrative in the Junius manuscript implies, and through this implication (re)creates, a unified, stationary and passive reader; instead, both texts are unconstrained by the fear of portraying more than a viewer could see at one time, from one place.

The Old English Riddles: Constructing the Speaking Object

Other poems depicting an individual's story of personal experience present similar interpretive problems. Difficulties in reading *The Seafarer*, like those facing the reader of *The Wanderer*, begin with and center around questions of unity of speech and placement of speech boundaries. *The Wife's Lament* and *Wulf and Eadwacer* each represent one female speaker's story. These poems have not initiated debate about the number of speakers and position of quotation marks, but their "incoherence" has provided the occasion for many critics to supply their own structures of narrative logic. The voice in each of these poems has an identifiable source, but that persona is not elaborated to represent a psychologically whole character. History, motivation, and location are all both detailed and vague. As in *Deor*, specific, complete stories seem to lie behind the poems, but the narrative gaps must be filled by the reader who either already knows the story or solves the poem as if it were a riddle. In none of these personal poems of experience does a complete story unfold from an identifiable location before the eyes of the reader.

The Exeter Book riddles in which a first-person speaker describes "itself," and then challenges the reader to guess its name, foreground the question underlying *The Wanderer* and other first-person poems: who is speaking? The object's (or creature's) identity is constructed in the riddle through the speaking of its history and the depiction of its world. This identity is not represented as being stable and unified; the object/creature goes through transformations, and the reader, glimpsing facets of its world, witnesses contradiction and change. Multiple and unusual vantage points—rather than a fixed position within the poem's fiction[55]—are offered to the reader who is challenged to make sense (meaning) of the text.

Like other Old English poetry consisting primarily of first-person speech, the riddles each represent the experience of a single "character." If that character (an object or creature in the riddles) had and offered a unified, comprehensive view of its world, the reader would adopt a perspective in relation to that view. Instead, like the wanderer who presents only tableaux, the speaker of a riddle describes its environment in an elliptic, fragmented way.

Often the reader is asked to see the object or creature here and there, then and now, in a variety of sometimes contradictory guises. A "horn" (riddle No. 14)[56] creates images of itself in a hall, on a battlefield, being carried across a border district and across a sea, and lying on boards (perhaps a table). The presentation of these various locations is punctuated by "hwilum," but the reader follows the horn back and forth between the scenes of hall and battlefield, so that "hwilum" serves only to suggest time periods not to impose a chronology upon them. Just as the reader cannot explain the shifting location by temporal progression, she or he cannot see the different scenes as backdrops for specific functions; the horn can be a drinking vessel or a musical instrument in the hall ("hwilum mægða sum minne gefylleð / bosm beaghroden; hwilum ic on bordum sceal, / heard, heafodleas, behlywed licgan" [8–10]; "hwilum ic gereordum rincas laðige / wlonce to wine" [16–17]), and it can be a musical instrument in the hall or on the battlefield ("Hwilum folcwigan / on wicge wegað, þonne ic winde sceal / sincfag swelgan of sumes bosme" [13–15]). The first location of the speaker—the place assigned to the past by verb tense—is not described; only by discovering that the speaker was on the head of an animal when it "wæs wæpenwiga" (1a)[57] does the reader finally solve the riddle. Locating the speaker "identifies" it in the sense of finding an answer for the riddle, but the horn is not represented as having one final, definable identity; rather, its different possible appearances and roles and the process of its identification are displayed.[58]

"Fish and River" (riddle No. 85) also presents the reader with the problem of locating the speaker, but rather than depicting several environments, it refers, in a cryptic way, to only one. In the first verse of the poem the speaker says that its dwelling place is not silent and still ("swige"); the reader is initially asked to imagine an unidentified creature in a particular, but only vaguely described setting. The project of the reader is to sketch in the details of that setting by identifying the other "person" of the poem with the dwelling place, and then to locate the creature within an environment necessary, on one level, to its existence and, on another, to its identification. As in the "Horn" riddle, the reader's perspective of the creature is a problem around which the mystery of the riddle gathers; it is precisely the dislocation of the reader that shapes the reading project.

Sometimes the speaker of a riddle asks the reader not only to see it in a variety of spatial and temporal locations but also to see "through its eyes"; the view of its world offered by the speaker is even less unified when it is refracted through the medium of that object's (mis)perception. The horn, speaking in what may be either of its guises (drinking vessel or wind instrument), says "sometimes people kiss me" (3b), and as a wind instrument, understands itself to swallow the wind from someone's breast (14b,15). A bow (riddle No. 23) believes that it swallows and then spits out poison (8–9).[59] If the reader were witnessing these actions directly, rather than "misunderstanding" them along with the speaker, she or he would see people drinking from a cup, someone blowing a horn, and a bow being loaded with and then shooting arrows. Instead, however, of seeing the speaker objectively (as the object that in one sense it is), the reader is now understanding it subjectively (from its point of view, as a subject). In most cases, the speaker represents "itself" as acting, rather than as an object acted upon (as swallowing, rather than being blown into; the exception is the horn being kissed rather than being drunk from). As a subject the speaker is like the reader; it performs human actions and speaks about its performance. Simultaneously, the reader approaches the speaker (aligns her or his view with its) and the speaker approaches the reader (shares her or his human attributes). The reader is never offered a distant, stable position from which to observe the object of her or his perception.

As the compound "reordberend" ("one gifted with speech," "a man")[60] attests, speech is a characteristic that can distinguish humans from non-humans in Old English literature; in the riddles, though, the human ability to speak is an attribute shared by all of the objects and creatures.

Critical theory that follows Freud and Saussure, by way of Lacan, describes humans as "speaking subjects" (rather than as "individuals"). From either an Anglo-Saxon or a post-structural point of view the idea of a "speaking object" is provocative and rich in contradiction. A crucial moment in the child's constitution as a subject is her or his entry into language. Catherine Belsey summarizes one statement of this principle:

> As Emile Benveniste argues, it is language which provides the possibility of subjectivity because it is language which enables the speaker to posit himself or herself as "I", as the subject of a sentence . . . it is only by adopting the position of the subject within language that the individual is able to produce meaning.[61]

The "individual," then, does not have a distinct identity prior to the moment of speaking, an identity which she or he simply conveys to others through speech; instead, speaking places her or him as a subject and suggests a (provisional) identity. To speak in the first person, taking for oneself the position of subject of the sentence, is not merely to follow a grammatical convention.

In the Old English riddles the process of constructing identity through speech is performed by nonhuman subjects. The "Magpie" riddle (No. 24) explicitly focuses on the association of voice and identity. The bird displays herself in various guises through her description of the sounds she makes;[62] her different voices indicate a lack of unity in the subject, a potential for change:

> Ic eom wunderlicu wiht,   wræsne mine stefne,
> hwilum beorce swa hund,   hwilum blæte swa gat,
> hwilum græde swa gos,   hwilum gielle swa hafoc . . .   (1–3)[63]

The magpie identifies herself, and the reader identifies the magpie, through her voice and particularly through its changes. The two subjects—magpie and reader—are alike in that they can speak about themselves. Most of the poem is constituted of a description of the bird's voices, but in the last four lines her name is represented in written (runic) characters, the significance of which the magpie explains: "Nu ic haten eom / swa þa siex stafas sweotule becnaþ" (9–10). One translation of "sweotule becnaþ" would be "manifestly signifies," perhaps indicating a difference between spoken and written depiction. Representation (of self) in writing, as in speech, is a specifically human activity, so again, the creature, by entering language, is making herself a subject; as she speaks, she inscribes her identity into the poem.[64]

Simply to consider the object or creature as speaking, though, would be to overlook a significant contradiction in the riddles: the speakers, whether they admit this or not, are not capable of speech. The contradiction indicates that the source of the riddle's speech both is and is not the represented speaker, that there is a fracture in the speaker's identity. For Lacan, as the subject enters language she or he is inevitably "split":

> The mirror-phase, in which the infant perceives itself as other, an image, exterior to its own perceiving self, necessitates a splitting between the 'I' which is perceived and the 'I' which does the perceiving. The entry into language necessitates a secondary division which reinforces the first, a split between the 'I' of discourse, the subject of the *énoncé*, and the 'I' who speaks, the subject of the enunciation.[65]

When, in the riddles, a speaking "object" says it cannot speak, the split in the "subject" is apparent.[66] The subject of the *énoncé* cannot speak, but the subject of the enunciation can. In riddle No. 60, the reed pen (the subject of the *énoncé*, or the "I" of the discourse) describes itself as "muðleas," and yet the voice surrounding this adjective in the text says that it "sceolde / ofer meodubence . . . sprecan" ("should speak over the meadbench"); this second voice can be understood as the subject of the enunciation. Both are the grammatical subject(s) of the clause, brought together through apposition. By drawing attention to speech, a characteristic fundamental to the difference between nonhuman and human (both of which describe the riddle "subjects"), the riddles emphasize lack of coherence. If the poem were read aloud before an audience the contradiction would be even more apparent.[67]

One interpretation of the speakers' inability to speak has been proposed by Marie Nelson who suggests that the composers of the riddles were working against the restrictions of a linguistic system based on binary choice and would not be bound by distinctions such as human or nonhuman.[68] This interpretation depends on the existence of such a binary system and the poets' knowledge of it. Perhaps, instead, the Old English language—its vocabulary and syntax—did not depend upon and cause binary thinking. In either case, the Old English riddles frequently present both choices and particularly display a merging of the positions of subject and object. The objects and creatures of the riddles are subjects in that they speak about themselves using the first-person pronoun, subjects in the active roles they assume, but they sometimes describe themselves in object positions. The speaker's identification occurs through its telling of a history of transformations throughout which it sometimes acts and sometimes is acted upon. "Leather" (riddle No. 12) was an ox treading and tearing the earth during its life (1–2), then was used in its various functions as a tool after its death. Even as leather, though, it performed active roles, giving drink to a warrior (5–6), and serving lords (15). "Reed Pen" (riddle No. 60) as an object was first played about (or "enclosed") by the waves (6–7), then was pressed by the point of a knife and by the hand and intention of a person (12–14); yet at the same time it speaks at the mead table (8–9) and announces messages (15–16). The identification of the riddle speakers involves questioning and playing with an either/or way of thinking that would ultimately place them in fixed categories.

Such a disregard for any delimitation of subject and object positions suggests a relationship between reader and text unlike that which is conventionally defined. An empirical model of reading casts the text in the role of object to be discovered by the reading subject. The text, though, is not an empirical object, already existing "out there," full of meaning, waiting only to be appropriated by a reader.[69] Gadamer's theory of the "fusion of horizons" of reader and text describes the subjective conceptualization at work in the process of understanding, as well as the text's active function in that process. The pretense of "objective" interpretation is undermined leaving no safe distance (no space free of prejudice) between the interpreter and that which is being interpreted. As is especially apparent in the riddles (but is also true of *The Wanderer* and the Junius drawings), the text only gains meaning through the reading process; the subject (reader), who has her- or himself been constructed through language, constructs the text. Questions of identity in the riddles revolve around a lack of subject/object categorization and around shifting perspectives of and on the speaker. By describing these problems within the text, a way of reading that does not presume for the reader a fixed subject position can be imagined.

The Dream of the Rood: Locations of the Cross's Voice

The Dream of the Rood in its opening section (1–27) resembles a second type of riddle wherein the speaker is not the riddle object itself but an intermediary (situated "between" object and reader) who describes aspects of that object's identity.[70] Although the reader of *The Dream* cannot immediately identify the described object, she or he can find multiple viewing positions by identifying with the dreamer; the dreamer offers a source of perception, and along with him the reader witnesses an enigmatic, changeable object in various and obscure settings. After the dreamer has provided a vivid description of the object's physical appearances, tracing its movements and transformations, the moment of the object's speech could be the occasion of self-identification; the cross, however, reveals its identity only indirectly, through the telling of its history, a process that unsettles the reader. The identifiable, although fluctuating, perspective offered by the dreamer is lost when the object begins to speak, describing itself in various locations and guises without, for a while, giving its name.

As in the first type of riddle (such as "Reed Pen," "Leather," and "Magpie"), the speech beginning at line 28 is represented as originating from the object whose identity is in question. Although *The Dream* is not explicitly concerned with naming this mysterious object, questions of the reader's points of view, the unique perspective suggested by the nonhuman speaker,[71] and the distinction of subject and object are raised through the cross's speech. Locating the object is not a problem; it clearly describes itself as being moved from its place of origin at the edge of a forest (29–30) to a hill (32b), where it remains fixed throughout the crucifixion (38b and 43b) and burial of Christ (71a), until it is buried in a deep pit (75a). These scenes occur in narrative sequence, but the reader does not passively observe their unfolding. The way in which the story is recounted, as in the following description of Christ climbing onto the cross as gallows, implies that the reader moves and witnesses events from different places:

> Ongyrede hine þa geong hæleð,   (þæt wæs god ælmihtig),
> strang ond stiðmod.   Gestah he on gealgan heanne,
> modig on manigra gesyhðe,   þa he wolde mancyn lysan.
> Bifode ic þa me se beorn ymbclypte.   Ne dorste ic hwæðre
>   bugan to eorðan,   (39–42)[72]

Although the cross is speaking, the scene is not, at first, subjectively described; Christ is seen from somewhere else as he mounts the gallows/cross, object of the sentence. The place where the speech originates is not the place from which the scene is viewed, and yet lines 39–41 are within the section of the poem representing the cross's description of its experience.[73] The object does not speak and see from the same position and no particular location is designated as the reader's vantage point.[74] The following sentence, however, reintroduces the cross as subjective speaker; the binding of Christ to the cross is "misperceived" by the speaker and the reader as his active embracing of the cross.[75] Within these few lines the reader moves from some unspecified place, at a distance from the speaking object and the portrayed scene, to the position where the subjective speech originates. There is an ambiguity in the representation of place in *The Dream*. The narrative occurs in precisely defined settings, but the reader is not securely placed in relation to these; instead, he or she moves through several points of view, some of them undefined.

The reader is not placed within the text's description; neither is she or he located as subject in opposition to the text as object. As in the riddles, a

merging of these two positions occurs when the object speaks and performs human actions; this confusion of roles is reflected in the method of
reading that the poem invites. The cross casts itself a subject and object,
sometimes in the same breath: "Gestah he on gealgan heanne. . . . Bifode
ic þa me se beorn ymbclypte" (40–42).[76] It can refer to itself as "ic," "unc,"
or "hit," a use of pronouns that reveals and creates the enigma of its
identity. If the pronoun "I" has not only grammatical significance but also
marks a crisis in the subject's identity, the cross binds itself to, and identifies itself with, another when it says "Bysmeredon hie unc butu ætgædere"
(48a). At this moment, it does not place itself as a distinct individual but as
one of two. I have suggested that Old English poetry, produced in a community-oriented culture, draws into question our notion of a border—a
clear distinction—between self and others. The cross is represented as
acting not according to its own judgment, but following the will of another, just as a retainer follows the will of his lord.[77] The impulse for its
actions lies outside itself. The identity of the cross further shades into that
of Christ as their experiences merge: the stories of their suffering, burial,
and ascent are identical. If the cross were not clearly designated as the
source of speech (if *The Dream* were as difficult to read in this regard as
The Wanderer), descriptions of experience such as "Þurhdrifan hi me mid
deorcan næglum" (46a) and "Feala ic on þam beorge gebiden hæbbe /
wraðra wyrda" (50–51a) could just as easily be assigned to Christ. A particular conception of self, formulated according to an identification with
others/community is indicated in the cross's speech and is emphasized by
the dual pronoun.

The dual pronoun embraces not just self and other but human (Christ
in his humanity) and nonhuman; both are being acted upon, sharing the
same experience, so that the cross represents itself very explicitly as a
human sufferer. In its interpretation of its story, though, the cross speaks
of itself as "hit" ("hit is wuldres beam" [97b]). As in its depiction of Christ
climbing the high gallows (40b), the speaking subject displays a split in its
identity; it simultaneously exhorts the dreamer (and/or the reader) to action in a very direct and immediate way ("hæleð min se leofa" [95b]), and
looks at itself from a distance of time and place. The cross transforms
itself, as it speaks its story, from subject to object, sometimes occupying
both positions at once, and sometimes binding its identity to Christ's.

The riddle of the speaker's identity in *The Dream* would seem to end
when the cross announces "Rod wæs ic aræred" (44a), yet this statement
does not mark a final moment when identification is complete. As in the
riddles, reaching a solution is only one part of the reading process. It is
not a privileged place of culmination, the goal to which the whole text was
directed; instead the poem dwells on the object's potential for change and

its manifold identities. Since the riddles do not contain their solutions, we are free to imagine that discovery would mean completion; *The Dream* shows that this is not so by continuing beyond the speaker's self-revelation. The cross names only one aspect of itself—one role it has played—and then continues to transform as it tells its history. The reader watches these changes (sometimes sharing the cross's perspective and sometimes observing from a distance) and actively participates in the poem's meanings, drawing on her or his previous knowledge of the story.[78] The text is not a delimited, independent object but the representation of a process of speech and identification which leaves room for the reader's act of producing meaning.[79]

Both *The Dream* and the "Chalice" riddle (48) contain the speech of an object within a description of that object spoken by another person, an observer. In these poems the voice framing the object's speech mediates through its description and, more obviously, through the instruction it provides to the reader; both speakers tell the reader how to interpret and act upon what the object has said. While the voice of the cross is an important element in *The Dream*, the introductory description of the chalice is primarily concerned with the silence of that speaking object; the ring speaks "torht butan tungan" (2a), it does not cry with "hludne stefne" (2b–3a), "strongum wordum" (3b). In an elliptical way the riddle directs the reader to the discovery that the object's "speech"—"Gehæle mec, helpend gæsta"—is actually a written inscription. Oral and written representation converge, occur simultaneously, in the play of the riddle.[80] Jewelery, weapons, crosses, and other artifacts were often engraved with some identifying information; this may have been the name of the craftsman (such as the inscription on the early eleventh-century Brussels cross: "Drahmal me worhte"),[81] the name of the person who commissioned the work (e.g., the gold frame of the ninth-century Alfred jewel is engraved: "Ælfred mec heht gewyrcan"), or a description of the material from which the object was made (e.g., runes on the eighth-century ivory Franks casket read: "hronæs ban").[82] The inscription on the riddle chalice is not as explicitly concerned with the identification of its bearer as are some of these engravings, but in the context of the riddle, it becomes a crucial element in naming the mysterious object. Described in the "Chalice" riddle are two ways in which an object could speak and identify itself: in the manner of other riddle objects as they construct their identity and also through inscription.

The speech of the cross in *The Dream* may also be understood as an inscription—a fixed text to be looked at, described, and explained. The framing voice of the observer may be imagined to describe, like the voice in the riddle of the chalice, the double image of a speaking and an inscribed object. The Ruthwell cross, as it is presently positioned, has north and south faces decorated with figural representations, each framed by Latin inscription (fig. 8), and east and west faces displaying an inhabited vinescroll pattern surrounded by Old English runic inscription (fig. 9).[83] The runes on the lower panels of the sculpture constitute a short poem that quite closely resembles part of the cross's speech in the Vercelli *Dream of the Rood*. Although the historical relationship between the sculpture and the poem is a matter of debate,[84] the fiction of *The Dream of the Rood* allows for a reading wherein the dreamer faces and interprets an inscribed sculpture, like the Ruthwell cross. To imagine such a situation is to sketch a conceptual framework for exploring methods of reading the runic inscription on the cross; thereby, the first-person narrative can be considered as represented in different contexts and according to different modes of description.

Beginning with "geredæ hinæ god almegttig" ("Almighty God stripped himself"), the worn and damaged Ruthwell inscription[85] speaks of the cross's experience of the crucifixion in words that run roughly parallel to lines 39a to 64a of the Vercelli poem. The speech is only one of several voices that the sculpture represents; to discover the place of the cross's narrative within this polyphony is to encounter again the question of a

8. Christ on the Beasts. Ruthwell Cross, north face.

9. Runic inscription and vinescroll. Ruthwell Cross, lower section of west face.

reader's perspective in relation to a multifaceted text. The voices constituting the cross include depictions of biblical narrative, verbal description of these images, vinescroll pattern (which, although it does not tell a story, is not silent), and the runic Old English inscription that corresponds to a passage from *The Dream of the Rood*.

The depictions of biblical scenes, each framed by verbal description, decorate the north and south faces of the cross (fig. 8).[86] Each of these panels conveys an aspect of a larger, already known story, but the iconographic program of the cross does not suggest a linear narrative reading, nor does it point in any obvious way to a unifying theme.[87] In contrast to this composite structure of representation that has many points of reference beyond itself, the story told by the cross on the east and west sides of the sculpture is simple and self-referential. Each side consists of panels of vinescroll framed by the story inscribed in runes (fig. 9). The pattern does not speak about anything; it is an end in itself, a focus for the viewer's attention. Similarly, the poem, in which the cross describes its role in the crucifixion, attracts attention to the cross itself.[88] Through first-person speech, the cross represents itself as a speaker, and through its story it explains its existence as a symbol. Together the vinescroll pattern and the poem arrest the viewer's thoughts on the medium itself, the sculptural text.[89] The cross's speech is directly represented only in the poem, but the cross as sculpture addresses the viewer through all of its imagery and inscription. Some of these voices direct attention away from the cross and toward other narratives, while others attract attention to the object.

When the cross tells its story, it represents itself as the source of that speech; the poem on the sculpture could be contained in quotation marks (as is the corresponding section of the Vercelli poem in modern editions) since the speaker is imagined as being an individual who, despite difficulties of representation, can be identified. The origin of the Latin inscriptions, though, is not identified; whoever speaks them—there may be several sources—is absent and uses a third-person mode of description. The Latin inscriptions efface their source with the result that the speaker (the medium between the viewer and the stories) is overlooked. Two disparate forms of speech, each with distinct implications for the viewer, are represented on the sculpture. If the voices speak to each other, if they correspond in some way, neither the sequence of their dialogue nor the nature of their interrelationship is defined.[90] Since the lowest panel on the south side depicts the crucifixion, the two types of speech can be read as converging narratively in their representations of this scene. The overlap though, is restricted to the level of narrative; the two voices speak about the crucifixion from different perspectives, offering distinct points of view.

Neither type of speech is authoritative, having priority over the other, but each provides for the other a context—a frame of reference. The poem, in which the cross represents itself as a medium, introduces—prepares the reader for—the figural depictions of the north and south faces; in the reading of this particular cross sculpture, the poem can be understood as coming first and describing a context for what follows. Yet, on a more general level, the cross's speech only has meaning within the larger narrative of Christ's life, the narrative suggested by the scenes and descriptions on the north and south faces. According to such a reading, the poem—the speech of a particular individual—is contained and defined by the story that the depictions—not bound to any authorial voice—represent. The voices emanating from the cross indicate the complexity, not the coherence, of their source.

The different contexts of the cross's speech in the Vercelli poem and on the Ruthwell cross implicate the reader in different processes of interpretation. In the manuscript poem the first-person speech is mediated by the dreamer's address to the reader; within the fiction of the poem, it is the dreamer to whom the cross speaks. For the reader of the sculpture there is no mediating voice; instead, she or he is in the place of the dreamer—directly in the presence of the cross, listening to its story. In such a situation there can be no mystery about the identity of the speaking object. While the identity of the speaking cross in the Vercelli poem is constructed through its speech and explicated through the speech of the dreamer, the identity of the first-person speaker represented on the Ruthwell cross is, in one sense, immediately apparent. The inscription reinforces the object's identity, drawing attention to the medium of representation; it does not construct an identity in the absence of the speaker. The difficulty in reading the sculpture comes when it is considered in its entirety, when one questions the place of the first-person, direct speech within the chorus of voices. In this sense, the "I" of the sculpture is more difficult to interpret than the cross's speech in the manuscript poem since the latter is carefully encased within layers of description.

The question of the reader's perspective has a literal meaning when asked concerning the position(s) from which the sculpture may be read.[91] When first constructed, the Ruthwell cross stood in a remote region of Northumbria and (some scholars speculate) designated a place of worship. The cross, like the speaker of a poem and her or his story, was the center, the focus, of a gathering. Éamonn Ó Carragáin argues that the sculpture's position and orientation would have had religious significance for a monastic community.[92] By analogy with another Northumbrian sculpture, the Bewcastle cross, which stands in its original location, scholars have suggested that the Ruthwell cross once had its principal face looking west.[93] During mass, when the worshippers stood to the west of the cross and faced east, the image of Christ standing upon two beasts—the largest image on the west face of the cross—would have dominated their view (fig. 8).

This image and its inscription ("IHS XPS IVDEX AEQVITATIS: BESTIAE ET DRACONES COGNOUERVNT IN DESERTO SALVATOREM MVNDI") evoked many spiritual concepts, some of which were enhanced by the temporal situation of the viewing and others by its physical situation (the position of the image in the east).[94] At other times, different images and inscriptions would have been the focus of the monks' attention, depending upon the specific situation—the time of day, the liturgical hour, the season. Each image, though, would always have had multiple significance; its meanings within many different contexts would have been present simultaneously to the viewer despite the predominance of one association at that specific time.[95] Even a single image when read by only one viewer, said several things at once. When that viewer moved and saw different images, patterns, and texts, the potential meanings of the sculpture would increase; they would multiply again when several viewers, each with his or her own perspective and interpretation, gathered around the cross. Nothing about the sculpture directed the readers to find a resolution for the differences between these perspectives. In its physical and interpretive situation, the cross—an object having multiple significance—was the focus of a community. Like a storyteller, the cross drew together an audience who gathered in its presence. The cross's story is really many stories at once, and these change through time. The multifaceted narrative is at the center of a community.

The difficulty of interpreting the Old English poems that depict personal experience through first-person discourse (e.g., *The Wanderer, The Seafarer*, and *The Wife's Lament*) has often been acknowledged. In order to make sense of these poems critics have constructed (often very imaginative) contexts for them and have allocated them to the genre of "elegy." Through this practice they have made the poems conform to the expectations and interpretive methods of a modern reader. Instead, recognizing that first-person speech is a structure common to poems like *The Wanderer*, the riddles (by definition difficult to interpret), and *The Dream of the Rood*, I have attempted to understand the poetry in terms of concepts (or conceptualizations) of identity. Since Old English poetry representing first-person speech resists our conventional reading practices, I have turned to recent theories of subjectivity and subject position—theories that challenge our preconceived notions of narrative and characterization—in order to trace a more appropriate interpretive practice.

CHAPTER 2

Peripheral Meanings:
Frames in Old English Poetry and Anglo-Saxon
Manuscript Illumination

When first-person speech is not represented in the expected manner,
the reader becomes disoriented. The voice of a character "should" help the
reader to recognize her or his own individuality and thereby provide the
reader with an identity in relation to the text. Paul Ricoeur locates narrative voice at the place where reader and text meet: "Voice . . . is already
involved in the problems of communication, inasmuch as it addresses itself to a reader. It is therefore situated at the point of transition between
configuration and refiguration, inasmuch as reading marks the point of
intersection between the world of the text and the world of the reader."[1]
According to this conception, a character's voice is crucial to the reader's
project of making meaning; it can provide a stable place from which comprehension is possible. If, instead of mediating between the two worlds in
order to facilitate understanding, the voice itself becomes a source of confusion, the whole conventional structure of reading begins to give way.

Like the representation of voice, frames are a place of mediation between the reader and the text. The interpretation of a poem or a picture
can be guided by framing devices that indicate a focus for the reader's
attention. Frames in Old English poetry and Anglo-Saxon art, like first-
person speech, work against their expected function, suggesting that our
conventional methods of interpretation are not appropriate and we must
read differently. The borders of Anglo-Saxon manuscript illuminations are
highly decorative and elaborately structured; they rival the illustrations
that they surround for the attention of the viewer. The intricate structure
of Old English poetry also includes framing devices that articulate the
limits of narrative or descriptive passages; like the illuminated borders of
Anglo-Saxon manuscripts, these poetic frames are elaborately crafted and
attract (as well as direct) the reader's attention.

When I speak of a frame (or a framing device) I am using that term in its broadest meaning. A frame is at once a picture frame, a line drawn around an image, a linguistic unit that introduces or concludes a passage of poetry, a frame of film, a context within which something has meaning, a frame of reference, a set of assumptions: all of these frames are places of mediation. Their expected function is to delimit that which is to be focused upon, distinguishing it from its "less important" surroundings and guiding the reading project; they mediate, then, between the general and the specific, and between the reader and the text. They shape an identity, often directing the reader's gaze away from the "inessential," away from the peripheral (the frame itself), and onto the primary subject matter.[2] A frame, like the speech of a character, can situate the reader; Jacques Derrida describes frames as being constituted of "point of view and a certain relation to the ideal limit."[3] Again, perspective and identity are related concepts since that which mediates can delimit the identity of the text by telling the reader to observe it from a certain point of view.

The Elaboration of the Frame

Frames conventionally play a supporting role in the making of meaning, and remain unobtrusive while doing so. Because frames in Anglo-Saxon art and Old English poetry are so conspicuous, they raise questions regarding methods and concepts of reading; these frames do not recede into the background while directing the reader to become absorbed in the meaning that they contain. The borders of manuscript illuminations illustrate vividly the elaboration of the frame and the nature of its mediation. The Book of Durrow (fig. 10), a Northumbrian manuscript dating to the mid-seventh century, has colorful, interlace borders which are not unobtrusive but capture the viewer's attention.[4] The lion representing St. John (according to a pre-Jerome symbolism) is surrounded by a frame with which it harmonizes in color and texture. Both figure and frame are colored with yellow, green and red. The interlace in the upper and lower borders corresponds to the curved yellow lines of the lion's body; the circles described by the winding interlace encompass a design of interlocking straight lines, just as, within its outline, the body of the lion is decorated with a geometrical diamond pattern; and the dots within the interlace ribbons of the side borders create a texture that is seen again in the face and stomach of the lion. The frame performs its function of delineating a space for the image, a space distinct from the rest of the manuscript page. It also adorns the figure of the lion, announcing that the image deserves

10. Symbol of St. John. Trinity College Dublin MS 57, fol. 191v.

attention. The reader does not, though, read this frame as being "mere" ornament, existing to advance the significance of the figure, but as a finely crafted pattern that arrests the gaze. The figure, rather than referring to a "real" lion (or even to a traditional representation of one), becomes ornamental and refers to its frame. Through their compositional similarities, figure and frame are read as having comparable significance; neither has priority over the other.

The border of the St. Mark carpet page in the Lindisfarne Gospels (fig. 11; written and illuminated between 687 and 721) lacks the decorative panels seen in the Book of Durrow; instead, such panels constitute the "main" text of this page of decoration. This frame intrigues the viewer in a different way. In the center of each side of the frame are two animal heads

11. St. Mark carpet page. London British Museum, Cotton Nero D.IV, fol. 94v.

joined to each other by a knot of interlace formed by their tongues. One has to look carefully at the frame's corner embellishments to realize that within the tangle of colorful ribbons are the haunches and wings of the creatures. The sides of the frame, then, must be composed of the bodies of these zoomorphs. While the "carpet" itself offers viewers the enjoyment of its richly colored panels of linear design, the border involves them in solving its visual puzzle. It challenges them as if with the question posed by the Exeter Book riddles: "ræd hwæt ic mæne" ("interpret what I mean"). The verb "rædan" is virtually unique among verbs for reading in other languages in that it includes in its semantic range the concepts of "reading a text," "solving a riddle," "explaining something obscure," and "discovering meaning."[5] The frame addresses the viewer and asks to be "read" in the Old English sense of the word; it illustrates that even that part of the text which seems peripheral must be read, and that reading involves solving a puzzle.

In the St. Mark symbol page of the Echternach Gospels (fig. 12),[6] the frame seems at once to fix the figure of the lion in position and to be exceeded by the animal. There is a dynamic relationship between the two, intensified at the places where figure and frame come into contact (the lion's nose, paws, and tail) or near contact (the inward extensions of the frame). The frame almost succeeds in determining the position of the lion, but the lion manages to disturb the symmetry of the frame and to trans-

12. Symbol of St. Mark. Paris Bibliothèque Nationale MS Lat. 9389, fol. 75v.

gress its limitations. While this illumination cannot be said to represent a "narrative" in the usual sense of the word, it is dramatic and demonstrates a relationship of border to depicted action wherein the border is a participant.

H. R. Broderick has described the "tangibility" of some illuminated borders in Anglo-Saxon manuscripts, citing the frame of the Chorus of Angels miniature in the Athelstan Psalter (fig. 13) as an example.[7] The creatures who exist outside the frame grasp it with their hands and bite its corners, drawing attention to its substance. Through the depiction of a world beyond the image, the spatial limitations of the representation become apparent, and that which is contained is portrayed as incomplete. This frame is also implicated in the narrative structure of the illumination. Some action and interaction is indicated among the choruses of angels and prophets: the characters gesture, share glances and perhaps words. The represented space is insufficient for the multitude, and those figures who are in closest proximity to the borders are seen as extending beyond that limit. The viewer imagines the "story" to continue past its border; the frame does not serve to limit the action.

The late tenth-century Benedictional of St. Æthelwold contains a Latin dedication recording that Bishop Æthelwold "commanded . . . to be made in this book many frames well-adorned and filled with various figures decorated with numerous beautiful colours and with gold."[8] This is the extent of Æthelwold's instructions. Such a description suggests that the decorative borders were at least as important to the bishop as the unspecified figures they would contain. The borders are composed of intricate acanthus leaf patterns within a solid gold periphery and are further embellished by elaborate corner rosettes (fig. 14). The colors, textures, and shapes of the frames are echoed in the images, and the figures, often located in close proximity to the borders, interact with them as if the borders shared the same narrative space. The frame of the Women at the Sepulchre miniature takes on a narrative function when it provides "wings" for one of the Maries, a groundline that delicately supports the three women, and a hiding place for one of the guards. At the same time, the image becomes decorative and refers to the frame when the guards' shields are depicted as being blue and green, and the stone upon which the angel is sitting as being pink. These are not mimetic colors but repetitions of the decorative colors of the border.

Such relationships between image and frame break down the division between representational and decorative elements of the composition; the two do not have distinct functions but work together to create meaning. The frame has a crucial effect on the narrative, since by its nature it functions to "screen out" contiguous events. At the same time, the borders in

13. Chorus of angels and prophets. London British Museum, Cotton Galba A.XVIII, fol. 2v.

the Benedictional suggest the continuity of the story. In the Women at the Sepulchre image, the situation of the Maries in the right border says that they have just arrived, and the viewer is urged to think about, to recall, where they have come from. Since the events of Christ's life depicted in the Benedictional would have been very familiar to its audience, the details that are omitted could easily be recollected. A frame structured in this way

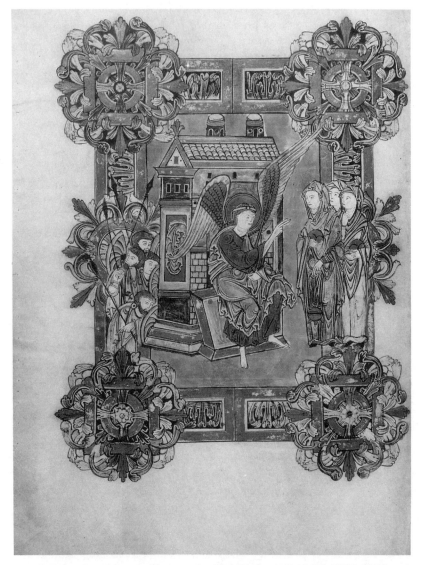

14. The women at the sepulchre. London British Museum, Add. MS 49598, fol. 51v.

does not ask the viewer to perceive the depicted moment as complete, but to imagine its continuation. Just as spatial continuity was implied by the frame of the Chorus of Angels miniature in the Athelstan Psalter, the reader of the depiction of the Women at the Sepulchre recalls the temporal extention of the narrative.

The representational and decorative elements of a pictorial composition can be designated by the terms "image" and "nonimage"; ordinarily, the frame would be thought of as a nonimagistic element of a composition containing a central image. An image is read as bearing a resemblance to something in the world beyond itself; conventionally, we associate image with the representation of "reality." Whitney Davis, in an article focusing on paleolithic art, questions "the context in which and the conventions by which a graphic pattern is taken to be an image of some reality."[9] He argues that there is nothing inherent about a pattern of marks that causes it to be an image, but that a particular pattern is interpreted (at first "incorrectly") as resembling something in the world, and then is repeated, with some variation, as a representation of that thing. Image-making is a process (recorded in palimpsests formed by cavepaintings) that begins with misinterpretation and continues by convention. The marks that are part of the drawing but are "not implicated in an image" may also have "semantic values" (132). Nonimage and image are relative terms: "For images, the depictive mark derives from seeing-as in relation to a nonimage mark" (133). What was once seen as image can through time become nonimage, and vice versa. He describes nonimage as "the most immediate and most important context of the image" and as "the unavoidable by-product of replicating the image"; it can change the image or bring about its decay (135–136).

Davis's work has implications for the understanding of representation and design (specifically, image and frame) in Anglo-Saxon art. In a manuscript illumination, the border would be expected to frame the image with nonimage, but also—on a more abstract, conceptual level—the creation and perception of image would be expected to occur within a context—a frame—of the recognition of nonimage. Some Anglo-Saxon illuminations seem to fit this description; the symbol page for the Gospel of St. John in the Book of Durrow (fig. 10) and for the Gospel of St. Mark in the Echternach Gospels (fig. 12) have nonrepresentational borders surrounding recognizable images. These nonimagistic borders have semantic value in relation to the image (as I have discussed above).[10] The distinction between image and nonimage in Anglo-Saxon art, however, resists definition in several ways. The pattern of lines that represents a lion in the Book of Durrow forms an outline around a nonrepresentational design. Physically, then, nonimage frames image that frames nonimage. Interpretively, the image does not refer to an external "reality"—a real lion—as much as to its nonimagistic frame; image does not detach itself from nonimage, but stresses its connection and concurrence with nonrepresentational pattern. Each book of the Grimbald Gospels[11] has an illuminated introductory page that depicts the evangelist's portrait and symbol. The borders of these illuminations consist of panels and medallions that contain images of human figures, angels, biblical scenes, the Trinity, and the Virgin and Child (fig. 15). Angels surround and support the medallions of the upper border, so that there is a repeated alternation between image and nonimage, neither absolutely containing the other. When the angels hold the frame and the figures within place their feet on its lower border, image embraces nonimage as part of its world. If the figure represents an angel, then the frame becomes a solid,

15. Portrait and symbol of St. John. London British Museum, Add. MS 34890, fol. 114v.

tangible bar because of its relationship to that figure. As in the illumination of angels and prophets in the Athelstan Psalter (fig. 13), where creatures grasp and bite the frame from a position outside of it, image provides an "immediate context" for nonimage, rather than the reverse (as described by Davis). Images in Anglo-Saxon manuscript illuminations are not simply defined against (in relation to) a backdrop of nonrepresentational patterns. The St. Mark carpet page of the Lindisfarne Gospels (fig. 11) best illustrates the problems of defining image through its relation to nonimage. Davis says that a pattern of lines begins to be perceived as an image when it is mistakenly "seen as" being the same as an object in the world. Through time, the mistake will be corrected ("disambiguation" will occur), but those lines in the pattern that caused the mistaken perception may be replicated because they do bear some resemblance to that object (122); in the replication, the lines will be interpreted as an image since, in relation to "nonimage marks," they can again be "seen as" representing something other than themselves (133). In the Lindisfarne carpet page, image frames nonimage while posing as nonimage. There is a reversal of the structure of nonimage framing image, whereby nonimage would be cast as the "unavoidable by-product," necessary but subsidiary to the creation and reading of image. This illumination, though, does more than merely subvert the expected relationship of representation and design; it plays with the recognition of image and nonimage, enticing the reader to repeat what Davis describes as the original "erroneous perceptual interpretation" (122).[12] What we first "see as" a frame is later discovered to be a stylized depiction of zoomorphs; instead of discovering that what appeared to be image is actually nonimage, the order of the process is reversed. At the same time, the zoomorphs represent nothing more than a frame, so they transform again into nonimage.

Davis's theory is helpful in that it stresses the role of interpretation in deciphering image. His evolutionary model, though, according to which nonimage precedes image and interpretation is "correctible" (119), is simplistic and not applicable to Anglo-Saxon texts. The St. Mark carpet page illustrates that the similarity of image and nonimage is not a mistake, corrected and forgotten, but a continually recurring challenge of interpretation. Davis's model does incorporate change, but what he describes as a progress occurring over centuries, as witnessed in palimpsests, is replaced in Anglo-Saxon illuminations by the coincidence of the apparently opposite modes, image and nonimage.[13] In Anglo-Saxon pictorial art, nonimage is not easily recognizable as such, providing the reader with a firm foundation upon which to establish, or a frame within which to perceive, the image; instead, it too must be deciphered and often constitutes what is central to the text.[14] Davis says that nonimage "is the very ground or possibility for change in the image, or, at the limit, for its decay altogether" (136); if nonimage is a threat, the Anglo-Saxon image is always endangered.[15] Several characteristics of Anglo-Saxon frames emerge from a comparison of frame/content to nonimage/image. There is no simple binary opposition between image and frame; nonimage, which can include frames, is often the most important aspect of an illumination; the frame (and all that it implies) is not rigidly defined, but can be both image and nonimage simultaneously.

Narrative Divisions and Locations of Meaning in Three Old English Poems

Frames participate in the construction of the reading process. The decorative borders of Anglo-Saxon manuscript illuminations relate to the images they contain in ways that complicate interpretation.[16] They do not advance the independent and finite meaning of a representation. Instead, they draw attention to themselves (so that the reader lingers in enjoyment of them and is aware of the text as something that has been crafted), and then, often, they overlap with the image, suggesting that the limit they have traced can be transgressed. The framing devices of Old English poetry construct a similar reading process, drawing attention to themselves and overlapping semantically with the passage they have defined. Like all frames, those of Old English poetry guide the reader's interpretation of the text (mediate between reader and text), telling her or him that this linguistic unit exists within a larger context, yet is in some way distinct from its surroundings (so they also mediate between general and specific). I shall describe three ways in which Old English poetic language may be framed: through narrative division (the marking off of a story within the story), through the repetition of words or ideas, and through the self-reference—self-description—of the language.

The Dream of the Rood is structured according to a complex series of narrative frames, beginning with the dreamer's address to the reader:

> Hwæt! Ic swefna cyst   secgan wylle,
> hwæt me gemætte   to midre nihte,
> syðþan reordberend   reste wunedon!   (1–3)[17]

After describing his vision of a tree, adorned with jewels but wet with blood, the dreamer tells us that he heard that tree to speak. Following this introduction is the cross's narrative, told from its own unique perspective, of the crucifixion. Before returning to the dreamer's closing exegesis and homily (addressed to the reader), the cross offers the dreamer its interpretation of the experience it has related. The poem is structured, then, so that the dreamer's speech to the reader frames that of the cross to the dreamer, and events portrayed as occurring in the present (the dreamer's act of speaking) frame those that occurred in the past. The structure of present framing past (especially when the return to the present is accompanied by a gain in knowledge, as in *The Dream*) is a classic one, still common in the narratives of novels and films. But in *The Dream* this structure is made more intricate by a series of inner frames, each existing at a different stage of the past. The dreamer's description of what he saw and then how he responded occur at a time that follows and enwraps the cross's speech; the cross's introduction to, and later its interpretation of, its story have their own temporal position, between the dreamer's speech and the cross's historical narrative.

The narrative frame of *The Dream of the Rood* resembles the borders of the manuscript illuminations in its intricacy and also in the way it performs the role of mediator between reader and text. The reader's attention is regularly brought back to the presence of the dreamer (and therefore to the presence of a framing discourse) by that speaker's self-referential remarks ("geseah ic" [14b, 21b, 33b, 51b]; "ic . . . ongytan meahte" [18]) and by the cross's addresses to the dreamer ("Nu þu miht gehyran, hæleð min se leofa" [78]; "Nu ic þe hate" [95]). The reader is always aware of the story as being mediated by the dreamer, just as the reader of a manuscript illumination does not overlook the frame but is attracted by its colors and design. The poem's elaborate and conspicuous frame does not simply guide our perception of the story it contains, but like the manuscript borders that are enjoyed through their relationship with the image, it responds to that story. Image and border, framed and framing text, do not exist independently. In *The Dream*, the inner story (the cross's narrative of the crucifixion and its interpretation of that narrative) has an effect on the next "level" of fiction (the dreamer's perceptions). The frame illustrates the way in which the cross's experience of the crucifixion affects a person to whom that experience is conveyed. It shows that the text has an effect on its context and does not exist in isolation. When a narrative frame displays an act of interpretation, the process of reading becomes the focus of attention. The external reader is not absorbed by the story's fiction but is aware of it as something that has been crafted and to which she or he will respond (as does the internal reader—the dreamer).

Two dreams are represented within the narrative of the biblical poem *Daniel*. They punctuate and are contained by the story of the fall of the

Hebrews and the rule of the Chaldeans. Like the dream in *The Dream of the Rood*, those of Nebuchadnezzar are surrounded by interpretation.[18] His first dream is introduced by a description of his pride—pride having previously led to the fall of the Hebrews. In it, he hears that the world will be made "oð edsceafte" ("to a new creation," 112b), that "rices gehwæs reðe sceolde gelimpan, / eorðan dreamas, ende wurðan" ("an end of each kingdom must cruelly occur, an end of earthly joy come about," 114–15).[19] When he awakens he is afraid and "ne [wat] word ne angin / swefnes sines" ("[knows] neither the word nor the purpose of his dream," 125–26). Discovery and interpretation become crucial; although the dream itself functions as a medium between God and Nebuchadnezzar, another stage of mediation is necessary before the text of the dream can possibly have an effect on the fictional world within which it occurs. Daniel's retelling and reading of the dream provide it with meaning. Reading frames the story both structurally (in that Daniel's interpretation marks the end of the dream sequence) and semantically (since the dream remains an unsolved mystery—described as "dygol" ["secret," 130a] and "wyrda gerynu" ["mystery of destinies," 149a]—until his reading makes it known). The king, like the dreamer in *The Dream of the Rood*, should respond to his dream, but despite Daniel's interpretation he does not. Nebuchadnezzar's failure to understand or even remember his dream may be construed as causing the failure of the interpretive frame in its mediation between text (dream) and reader (ultimately, the king).

Although the dream does not influence the king's life, for the listening or reading audience, it does have a significance that extends beyond a particular narrative moment.[20] In speaking of the fall of nations, the dream refers both back in time to the fall of the Hebrews and forward to the conquest of Babylon; it indicates a cyclic, repetitious pattern in history. The dream is a moment of heightened significance at which time, through remembrance and prediction, the course of history becomes manifest. It is a pause in the movement of time, distinct in its tempo from the events that surround it.[21]

Nebuchadnezzar's second dream is presented in a narrative structure similar to his first; interpretation precedes and follows it. Although the king had, for a time, believed in the Hebrews' God, he became too proud,

> oðþæt hine mid nyde   nyðor asette
> metod ælmihtig,   swa he manegum deð
> þara þe þurh oferhyd   up astigeð.   (492–94)[22]

The dream and Daniel's interpretation follow this statement of Nebuchadnezzar's pride. As Daniel's reading makes explicit, the king's vision of a radiant tree, overspreading the earth until it is cut down, signifies the exalted position of Nebuchadnezzar and his impending fall. The king is left in a state of fear, as he was following his first dream (after the first "him sorh astah" ["anxiety rose up in him," 118a] and following the second "him þæs egesa stod" ["fear of the dream confronted him," 524b]); again, he immediately seeks an interpretation. This vision, like the first, is a mystery that can only be deciphered by Daniel.

The portrayals of the king's reactions to the two dreams are similar: although he is impressed by the fact of interpretation, he does not act in response to the dream's message, so the dream does not extend beyond its interpretive frame and into his life. Nebuchadnezzar does, however, remember his second dream, and unlike the first, it is described vividly and interpreted with specific reference to subsequent events. While the first dream has wide implications, extending throughout the whole poem (and then beyond), the second is explicit and limited in its reference. The implications of the first dream are not spelled out for the (external) reader through Daniel's interpretation; in the poem we are simply told, "eode Daniel . . . swefen reccan sinum frean" ("Daniel went to explain the dream to his lord," 158–59). We can only imagine Daniel's reading, which may differ from ours. The second dream, though, is read through Daniel's very detailed interpretation. Our reading—our interpretive framework—is aligned with the reading portrayed within the text, and is verified when the experience of the king immediately echoes events symbolized in the dream; after history has unfolded as predicted, the dream is said to have been proved true ("swefn geseðed," 653a). Although both dreams are elaborately framed with layers of interpretation, the framing structures are not identical. Acts of reading are explicitly represented, and are seen to be complex in their demarcation and binding of different aspects of the text.

In the center of *Daniel*, between the two dreams, are two lyrics: the Song of Azarias and the Song of the Three Children. According to the design of the poem the dreams frame the lyrics, although they neither comment upon them nor strikingly resemble them in subject matter. It is within the context of the poem's temporal rhythms and kinds of signific....tion that the dreams resemble and focus attention on the songs. Like the dreams, the lyrics create a pause in the narrative flow. Narrative progress stops when the three children are thrown into the oven; it waits for Azarias's song of praise and prayer. Resuming briefly to describe the intervention of the angel, the narrative pauses again while the three children sing of the created world's glorification of God. Azarias's song recalls the pride and fall of the Hebrew nation, and then looks back further to God's promise to Abraham, Isaac, and Jacob; like the king's first dream, it is a moment outside of history that focuses attention on history's process. The second lyric has no temporal reference at all, but speaks of the timeless praise of God by all creation. Their difference from the story that surrounds them characterizes the lyrics as what Adeline Bartlett calls "independent medallions woven into the more or less narrative fabric,"[23] or what Mary Ann Caws describes as "framed moments," instances of "the other in the same."[24] Like the dreams, they are texts within the larger text, having their own condensed significance and requiring interpretation to link them to the narrative of the poem. Azarias's prayer is introduced by the explanation:

> Ða Azarias ingeþancum
> hleoðrade halig þurh hatne lig,
> dreag dæda georn, drihten herede . . . (279–81)[25]

When the song has ended, its completion is marked by a repetition of its purpose and a description of its results (the arrival of the angel). A narrator's voice encircles the song, talking about it and binding it to the narrative action.

The Song of the Children has a thicker frame. In a five-line introduction (356b–61) the unidentified narrator simply states that the three children of Israel praised, and asked all creation to praise, the eternal lord. The prayer is followed, though, by a more precise explication. A councillor who is wiser than Nebuchadnezzar—someone who is specifically "wordgleaw" ("wise in words," 417)—tells the king to consider, understand, and act upon what the children have said. The first dream was interpreted by Daniel so that "sona ongeat swiðmod cyning / ord and ende þæs þe him ywed wæs" ("at once the arrogant king understood the beginning and end of what was revealed to him," 161–62); now the councillor instructs the king to "ongyt" ("understand," 420) the subject of the children's song. The songs, like the dreams, are framed and mediated by interpretation—either that of an unnamed source directed to the reading audience, or that occurring within the fiction, offered by one character to another.

The scene with which the poem ends is also framed and distinct from its narrative backdrop. Like the dreams and the songs, the event of the angel writing on the wall comes as a surprise to the fictional characters within the poem and to the listening or reading audience. At the moment when Belshazzar, ruler of the Chaldeans, is most proud and boastful, the sign is given and his attitude is instantly changed. Bartlett describes lines 712–29 of Daniel as an example of "antithesis" (46); the king who was "bliðemod" ("cheerful," 712a) becomes "forht on mode" ("frightened," 724b) as the poem describes an abrupt shift from apparent and limited earthly power to the eternal, immeasurable power of God. Belshazzar's response to the event is much like Nebuchadnezzar's to the dreams and songs—he is "egeslic" ("afraid," 718a), "forht on mode" ("frightened," 724b), and "acul" ("terrified," 725a); his fear of the enigma leads to his search for an interpretation. The "tacen" (717a) that causes this crisis is a mystery that cannot easily be comprehended. A conceptual frame is formed by Daniel's reading of the message and its significance, an act of interpretation that is more literally a "reading" than the explication of the dreams and songs.[26] The angel's writing produces "baswe bocstafas" ("purple or red letters," 723a), "ærendbec" ("written messages," 734a). That the act of writing and its product have a reference that must be deciphered is indicated by descriptions such as "tacen" and "beacen" ("sign," 717a and 729a).[27] The inscription is also called "worda gerynu" ("the mysteries of words," 722b), and later simply "seo run" ("the mystery," 740b), linking this supernatural event to Nebuchadnezzar's first dream, which was described as "wyrda gerynu" ("the mysteries of the fates," 149a). Daniel is asked to interpret and explain ("arædde and arehte," 740a) what the mystery proclaimed. In this clause, the verbs have two objects, and two concepts of reading converge: "[H]e him bocstafas / arædde and arehte, hwæt seo run bude" (739b–40). Daniel is both reading a text ("bocstafas") and deciphering the implications of a mystery. Both activities create an interpretation that embraces a passage of special significance and brings about its inclusion in the narrative.[28]

At the outer borders of *Daniel* are two accounts of falls of nations. These typify the course of history as represented in the poem and are remembered or predicted when history is revealed in the dreams, songs, and mysteries. The fall of the Chaldeans mirrors that of the Hebrews in its details: pride overcomes both nations as they, acting in accord with the devil, indulge themselves with wealth and wine. The collapse of both states occurs when they are apparently securely established within the walls of well-fortified cities. The Hebrews are introduced as the possessors of a kingdom ("Gefrægn ic Hebreos . . . cyningdom habban," 1–3a) and the rulers of cities (9a); their principal city was secured with weapons and adorned with walls (38–41), and their possessions protected by fortifications (44a). Belshazzar, king of the Chaldeans at the close of the poem, is described as the lord of cities (676, 712b), and the Chaldeans are said to have possessed a kingdom ("cyningdom ahton," 679b); they lived, unafraid of attack, under the protection of walls that enclosed them (690, 695b-696).

It is precisely at these moments of seeming stability that destruction occurs. The Chaldeans lay waste the "winburh" of the Hebrews, rob the buildings of their treasures, and destroy ("abrecað") each of the fortifications that stand as protection for the Hebrews (57–64). In turn, the Chaldeans will be overcome by the Medes who plan to destroy ("abrecan") Babylon (686–90, 697–99). The scene of the angel's writing on the wall occurs within this final section of the poem. Three times it is stressed that the angel's hand reaches into the hall:

> Him þæt tacen wearð   þær he to starude,
> egeslic for eorlum   innan healle . . .   (717–18)

> þa þær in egesan   engel drihtnes
> let his hand cuman   in þæt hea seld . . . (720–21)

> Geseah he engles hand
> in sele writan   Sennera wite.   (725–26)[29]

The seemingly secure and solid structure is vulnerable; it can be penetrated. The outer frame of *Daniel*, then, consists of the collapse of established order, the crumbling of walls. The weakness or failure of enclosure depicted at the limits of the poem corresponds to a lack of narrative delimitation; instead of describing the completion of a chain of events, the final section of the poem represents history at the threshold of repetition. The narrator's reference to a time beyond the story's limits draws the reader's attention to events outside the scope of the narrative, and the imminence of the fall of the Chaldeans suggests an ongoing, cyclical pattern.[30] Neither the structures depicted in the poem—the fortified cities of the two nations—nor the structure of the poem are as stable and fixed as they would appear.[31]

Daniel is symmetrically structured with the dreams framing the songs, and the falls of the two nations encompassing the entire poem. It is like *The Dream of the Rood* in its precise balancing, its mirror image construction—and both poems also concern reading. The framing pattern of *The Dream*, however, depicts layers of discourse and interpretation, while that of *Daniel* consists of a series of events whose interrelationship is less clearly defined.

The dreams provide a context for the songs primarily in their tracing of a rhythm and a signification that are distinct from the poem's narrative. The falls resemble in subject matter the dreams that they encircle. For the external reader, they guide in the interpretation of the king's enigmatic visions: because the dreams, which refer elliptically to the end of earthly joys (114–15) and to the fall of a magnificent tree (510–12), occur within the context of the declines of two nations, we are able to delimit and comprehend their reference. The internal readers (Daniel and Nebuchadnezzar), lacking our wider perspective, are able to glimpse the course of history that envelops them by following the indications of the dreams. Frame and content have a mutual significance understood through interpreting their relationship. With the exception of the fall of the Hebrews, related in a direct way as an historical event, each of the narrative elements involved in the frame structure of *Daniel*—songs, dreams, and the fall of the Chaldeans—must be read and is itself framed by interpretation. The fall of the Chaldeans is predicted in a straightforward way by the narrator (678b–79), but is also the subject of the mysterious writing on the wall. *Daniel*, with its complex arrangement of frames, is structured around and by mysteries that require deciphering; it is a poem about reading as mediation.

Beowulf contains many stories within the story; some of these are like the dreams in *The Dream of the Rood* and *Daniel* in that they (should) serve the purpose of instruction. After Beowulf's victories over the monsters, at a time when the hero could become proud, Hrothgar tells him the story of Heremod, a Danish king who was at first a good and brave ruler but was overcome by pride and greed. At the conclusion of his speech Hrothgar advises Beowulf:

> Ðu þe lær be þon,
> gumcyste ongit!   Ic þis gid be þe
> awræc wintrum frod.   (1722b–24a)[32]

Hrothgar marks the limit of his story but also expresses his wish that the effect of the tale will be a force in Beowulf's career as a ruler—that the significance of the story will extend beyond the moment of its telling. Like the cross's story and the manuscript drawings that have an effect on their frames—either by influencing the frame's colors and design or by extending the narrative into the border—the stories told within *Beowulf* are not (self-)contained but pertain to the events surrounding them. Hrothgar offers Beowulf his story of Heremod as advice from one who is experienced ("se wisa," 1698b; "wintrum frod," 1724a; "blondenfeax" ["gray-haired"], 1791a). This story has all the characteristics that Walter Benjamin ascribes to tales related orally by storytellers: it communicates experience, provides counsel, and continues to unfold when it is received and responded to by the listener ("The Storyteller . . ."). Peter Brooks, in his article "The Storyteller," follows Benjamin and considers what happens when an oral story is represented in a written text:

> Narrating is never innocent, and the narrative that frames another allows the writer to dramatize the results of the telling. And this no doubt gives

a signal to the reader that the tale told can and should react on his own life: that literature is not inconsequential.[33]

The response of the listener occurs in the frame, and through that frame's drama, the reading process is shaped.

Hrothgar's story is told at a gathering in celebration of Beowulf's victory. Much of the storytelling depicted in the poem occurs in such a setting. The Finn episode is another story related at a time of rejoicing, and provides a focus for the description of a story's social context. A general situation of celebration and storytelling introduces and concludes the tale:

> Þær wæs sang ond sweg   samod ætgædere
> fore Healfdenes   hildewisan,
> gomenwudu greted,   gid oft wrecen,
> ðonne healgamen   Hroþgares scop
> æfter medobence   mænan scolde,
> [be] Finnes eaferum,   ða hie se fær begeat . . . (1063–68)[34]

>   Leoð wæs asungen,
> gleomannes gyd.   Gamen eft astah,
> beorhtode bencsweg,   byrelas sealdon
> win of wunderfatum.   (1159b–62)[35]

As our reading moves inward through the opening frame to the story, our attention becomes more focused until we arrive at the particular story chosen from all others. The narrative frame serves, then, to separate the specific from the general. The particular story told, though, is incomplete and allusive. In the Finn episode a tragic conflict between the Frisians and the Danes is told primarily from the point of view of its effects on two characters: Hengest and Hildeburh. The events are related in only a fragmentary way; the audience would have had to draw upon a previous knowledge of the story in order to make sense of the scop's tale. The tale of Finn is not contained within its narrative frame, but spills over, having reference beyond that limit. A similar "spilling over" is depicted graphically in the Women at the Sepulchre miniature of the Benedictional of St. Æthelwold (fig. 14). In both cases, the story in a larger form would have been familiar to the audience before that particular telling. The context necessary for understanding the related (or depicted) story—what came before and after, what has been left out—is held in the audience's memory. The story alludes to that memory, which becomes a conceptual frame for the narrative. Like a frame, the memory of narrative details, which surround the ones portrayed, shapes and gives meaning to the represented story. Because the narrative frame and the illuminated border quite obviously exclude something (this larger, conceptual frame), readers are aware of the frame's presence. They know something is missing and that they are involved in creating the meaning of the representation. What is absent from the story is made present through the reader.

In the case of a story—like the tale of Finn—told at a social gathering, the project of creating meaning is performed within a community of readers. This would have been a typical setting for the transmission of Old English poetry, which was once composed orally, and later, after the poems had been transcribed, continued to be read aloud to a group of listeners. Since the story alludes to narrative details held in the memories of all the listeners, it draws them together; they are all included, sharing the same frame of reference. The orally delivered poem would have depended upon the shared knowledge of a community of listeners for its meaning. The gaps in the narrative that allude to something beyond that particular telling implicate the readers in the construction of the text and make the text a gathering place for the community. The story would have been a focal point, reinforcing social bonds. While the general situation of storytelling (as represented in the fiction) is "screened out" at the moment when the story of Finn begins to be told (the other stories are left in silence), a context for the story is invoked through that tale's allusiveness. The frame does not separate the story from the general social context within which it occurs.

Perhaps because of the number of framed stories within *Beowulf*, or perhaps because the poem begins with story of Scyld, the relationship between the account of Beowulf's activities and the other narratives in the poem is difficult to determine. Typically, scholars have described the stories within the story as digressions or interruptions, but there is some disagreement as to where to draw the line between such diversions and the "main" story of the poem. For H. M. Chadwick, "incidents in the history of the royal families of the Danes and the Geatas" and "allusions to heroes of the past" "interrupt the action," which begins with Hroðgar's building of Heorot and ends with the funeral of Beowulf.[36] Fr. Klaeber explains in the introduction to his edition that

> the subject-matter of *Beowulf* comprises in the first place, as the main plot, three fabulous exploits redolent of folk-tale fancy . . . and secondly a number of apparently historical elements which are introduced as a setting to the former and by way of more or less irrelevant digressions.[37]

He includes in his list of "episodic matter" about 700 of the poem's 3100 lines (p. liii); this does not include the more than 1300 lines of speeches which, he says, often "contain digressions, episodes, descriptions, and reflections, and thus tend to delay the progress of the narrative" (p. lv). Adrien Bonjour follows Klaeber in his analysis of what is extrinsic to principal story of *Beowulf*.[38] Recently, H. J. Diller has challenged Klaeber's and Bonjour's "standard" list of digressions.[39] He begins his study by attempting a definition of "digression," and sees his analysis as less "impressionistic" than the others. Despite Diller's scientific approach—his drafting of categories and lists based on Roman Jakobson's linguistic semiotics—his argument is founded on several unquestioned assumptions, including the important one of what constitutes the "main" story.

Digressions are usually described as interrupting the poem's narrative flow. Both Diller and Eric Stanley note the illogic of applying such a label to the Scyld episode; Stanley objects (to Chadwick and Bonjour),

> but a narrative work cannot start with an interruption except in a strange, academic view which subjects literature to repeated re-reading and is forgetful of an important consideration in judging literature, at least secular, narrative . . . literature, that literature was written to be read or heard for the first time.[40]

Critical questioning of the concept of digressions in *Beowulf* begins, then, with the problem of the priority of place given to a subordinate episode. In Stanley's article, this questioning focuses on an Anglo-Saxon audience's perception of narrative structure. The relative importance of various aspects of the poem—of any text—have to do with expectations and methods of reading. Our standard notion of the main events of *Beowulf* can be understood as no more than a modern preconception, shaped and perpetuated by recent scholars. There is a narrative thread running through the poem, continually reappearing in the midst of the telling of various stories and histories, but this narrative is given priority neither structurally nor semantically.

Both Klaeber and Diller see the speeches in *Beowulf* that stray from their narrative context as being digressive; the story, as told by the unidentified narrator,[41] is what shapes the poem, and the speeches often deviate in their description of extrinsic matters. A narrative like that described by Klaeber and Diller is hierarchic; Mieke Bal compares this kind of text, constituted of a story containing characters' speeches, to a sentence structured by a syntactic design:

> The dependence of the actor's [embedded] text with regard to the narrator's text should be seen as the dependence of a subordinate clause to a

main clause. According to this principle, narrator's text and actor's text are not of equal status.[42]

In this model, grammatical indicators tell the reader which clauses contain the crucial information and which are merely supportive or descriptive of that information. Following but inverting Ball's analogy, I would suggest that the lack of hierarchy in Old English poetic syntax can be seen as corresponding to a leveling of discourse throughout the narrative. Phrases are given in apposition and descriptive layers accumulate without being ordered according to importance. Semantic units stand side by side in paratactic arrangement so that, rather than being guided by connectives, the reader determines the relationship between parallel sentences or clauses. When adverbs of time do occur, and apparently sort out the narrative's chronology, they are often ambiguous in meaning. "Þa" can mean "when," "then," "thereupon," "since" (even "there" or "where") and can be translated as a conjunction linking two equal clauses or as an adverb subordinating one to the other. "Siððan" can also function as either a conjunction or an adverb, meaning "then," "when," "since," "later," or "afterward."[43] Often, elements of the sentence are not defined as either being "dependent" or having major significance; neither are speeches (or other digressions) within the poem of unequal status to the narrator's telling of the story. Such structures, strange to the modern reader accustomed to a clearly articulated narrative progression, suggest that the Anglo-Saxon audience did not expect a single story to predominate, and all other aspects of the poem to be signaled as secondary.

Whether to consider all speeches in *Beowulf* as digressions is "a major problem" for Diller. He resolves that "since the speeches are events in the chain of events which make up the main story, they are by definition not digressions" (71). One obvious problem with this resolution is its assumption as a premise that a main story has been defined. More revealing of the nature of the problem of speeches, though, is one of his exceptions to this rule. A speech is a digression if during its delivery—as in the tale of Sigemund and Heremod—"the dividing line between what the author says and what the fictitious character says" is "wiped out" (72). When Diller speaks of the author, he means the unnamed narrator; his fusion of the two is indicative of the authority he gives to the voice of the narrator.

As long as the tale is contained within the speech of a fictitious character, it has a place within the context of the main story, but the controlling voice of the narrator contains the main story within which the "other" person's speech occurs, and it should not be led astray by the wanderings of that subordinate discourse. Diller is using the identity of speakers to support his definition of digressions. Since, as he admits (and as I have argued[44]), speech boundaries are not fixed, the basis for his categorization is not firm. All of the voices are fictional constructs, bound by the limits of the poem; none is represented as having the authority of being completely without context. The various aspects of the poem resist categorization. The problem of the speeches should not be smoothed over since it is symptomatic of the larger issue of interpreting the relationship between the center of the poem and its periphery.

Two attempts have been made to visualize the narrative structure of *Beowulf*, accounting for its digressions, by creating analogies with art. Adeline Bartlett describes the poem as a tapestry:

> I believe that the method of *Beowulf* is the method of all Anglo-Saxon epic; and I should prefer to characterize it as a tapestry, which presents its pictures in a series of panels. Each verse pattern is a panel or section of the storied tapestry. It has an organic unity of its own and it also has its place in the series of pictures (some of them narrative, some descriptive, some didactic) which tells a connected, unified story. At any given moment the poet may appear to be more interested in the elaborate detail than in the composition of the whole.[45]

"Pictorial and moralizing passages" she imagines as "independent medallions woven into the more-or-less narrative fabric, the ordinary patterns of which they definitely interrupt" (72). Through these images, she describes the paratactic structure of *Beowulf*; narrative is side-by-side with description, and different aspects of the poem are represented as being of equal importance. Her picture is also highly decorative, illustrating the value placed on design in Anglo-Saxon pictorial and poetic art.

Bartlett does not speak of specific examples of Anglo-Saxon art. John Leyerle draws an analogy between the narrative structure of *Beowulf* and the interlace designs that decorate Anglo-Saxon sculpture, jewelry, and manuscripts.[46] The episodes form narrative strands, while recurring topics (e.g., threats from monsters, visits to a hall, women as the bond of kinship) weave together to produce a thematic fabric. Like Bartlett, Leyerle argues that the poem is a unified whole: the episodes and thematic parallels do not detract from a distinct, principal story, but join together to create a complex, multifaceted text. Both Bartlett's image of a tapestry and Leyerle's of interlace design give equal value to all aspects of the poem; Leyerle concludes, "there are no digressions in *Beowulf*" (13).

Besides narrative and thematic threads, Leyerle describes an interlace pattern within the sentence, woven of phrases or words in variation; he considers this type of interlace to be merely "decorative," not "structural" like that woven of narrative or thematic strands. Ultimately, he makes a distinction between structural interlace, as found in textiles, narrative and thematic texts (this interlace is essential to its product: "unravel the threads and the whole fabric falls apart" [8]), and the (relatively superficial) decorative interlace of manuscript illuminations and syntactic structure. I would argue, though, that in Anglo-Saxon art, decorative and narrative structures—representation and design—cannot be separated; the "two" create meaning together. Leyerle's evidence proves my statement. Because "cloth perishes easily and only a few fragments of Anglo-Saxon tapestry survive" (5), he must compare the structural interlace of narrative to the decorative interlace of manuscript illumination. A piece of cloth, however, if it had survived, would not have provided the analogy between *Beowulf* and interlace art that works so well with reference to manuscript illumination. The cloth would be held together, not by an elaborate interlacing of threads but by a simple binding of warp and weft.

The analogy that circumstances compel Leyerle to develop illustrates the elaborate decoration of Anglo-Saxon narrative. In order to clarify my response to his distinction I must refer to an argument I have already made: there is a corresponding significance between sentence structure and narrative structure. If variation within the sentence is purely decorative, then so is the presentation of narrative elements from a variety of perspectives, or if narrative interlace has meaning, then so does syntactic interlace. In fact, the substance of both sentence and poem are not separable from, but constructed of, elaborate patterns.

I would like to suggest another way of visualizing the narrative of *Beowulf*, one that speaks of a way of perceiving and understanding that corresponds to Old English poetic structure. Having described the function of the frames that mark off the internal stories of the poem, I return to the image of the framed illumination in order to question the place of these stories in relation to the whole poem. To introduce the concept of frames is to address the issue of what is central to the text and what is peripheral. The tapestry image places the aspects of the poem side by side, overcoming the imposition of a semantic hierarchy, and the interlace analogy achieves the same effect by picturing a pattern of alternation. Neither questions the meaning of the relationship between the various aspects of the poem. By referring to the image of a frame, I am focusing on the borders where the tapestry's panels meet or the folds where the interlacing threads overlap.

It would seem that the stories within the story are, by definition, framed rather than framing elements. Diller compares their topics to that of the "surrounding text" (73), and I have described the narrative frames that delineate them and distinguish them from what precedes and follows. Their meaning, then, would seem to be contained, to an extent, and given a context by the story of Beowulf's present exploits. The internal stories, though, also frame the text that contains them. Klaeber says that the historical digressions are "introduced as a setting" to the "main plot" (pp. xii–xiii) and Diller defines them as "telling or summarizing sequences of events outside the main story" (73). In these roles, the stories provide surrounding information, telling of events that lead up to or follow from the occurrences within the story of Beowulf or events that are in some way parallel to them. The stories in *Beowulf* can be compared to the images within the border of the Grimbald Gospel illumination (fig. 15). Individually they are framed, but together they create a frame for the representation of St. John. (This analogy has its limitations since the painting is restricted in a way that the poem is not: it cannot depict the smaller images as both central and peripheral simultaneously—they are situated at the painting's border.) When the stories in *Beowulf* are referred to as digressions or interruptions, the implication is that the stories are of secondary importance; so they are situated at the border of the text also in that they are extrinsic to what is considered crucial in the poem.

Frames, peripheral to the object of the reader's interest, are conventionally thought of as merely supportive of meaning. If the stories within *Beowulf* simply provided a setting for the "main plot" they would serve such a function. The frame constituted of these stories, though, is like the acanthus borders of the Benedictional of St. Æthelwold illuminations, or the narrative borders of the stories themselves, in its significance. The elaborate frames of the illuminations vie with the narrative depiction for the attention of the viewer, extending into that depiction and also referring outward to a larger, familiar narrative context. Both the manuscript page and the poem represent a narrative that can be distinguished by the reader from the surrounding elements of the composition. These borders shape and decorate the narrative but also have a substance of their own. Klaeber, as I have said, counts 2000 lines of digressions and (often digressive) speeches in the 3100-line poem. Wayne Dynes describes the "thickening of the frame elements" in Hiberno-Saxon art, which causes them to "rank, simply in terms of surface occupied, on a par with the depicted elements within the frame."[47] The stories in *Beowulf* and the borders of the illuminations occupy a large proportion of the composition and also of the reader's attention. Like the illuminated borders, the stories extend into and become entangled with the "central" representation—as when Hroðgar's story of Heremod continues beyond the time of its telling (and of its historical occurrence) and has an effect on Beowulf's future life. From the reader's point of view, it reaches into the "main" narrative as a negative model against which to measure Beowulf. The stories, like the Finn episode, are often more allusive than the narrative of Beowulf's life. Situated (semantically) at the edge of the poem, they are at the place where the text is most open to the audience. Like the border of the Benedictional's Women at the Sepulchre illumination (fig. 14), they mediate between text and reader—but by inviting the audience to participate in remembering omitted details (rather than by directing interpretation and defining meaning). The allusive stories are located at the border between audience and text and also at the limit between the part of the tale being told and the whole tale held in memory.[48] Although structurally they are contained and even framed within the poem, the stories function as a frame and do so in a way that specifically resembles patterns of framing in Anglo-Saxon manuscript illumination.

The stories within *Beowulf* have often been described as interruptions to the main plot, but this analysis is also based on the unquestioned assumption that priority should be given to narrative progress. Temporally, the stories, in their situation and significance, are both within and bordering upon the narrative of Beowulf's life. With reference to the linear depiction of that narrative, they are bound within a story and create a pause in its narration. Mary Ann Caws speaks of framed passages as being "privileged," and says they "are to be read against the flow of ongoing narration and the dispersion of life narrated and lived."[49] The tales told in *Beowulf*, shaped and ornamented by framing passages, can be described in this way—as intervals departing from, but caught within, the larger story. Storytelling occurs at special moments, occasions (often celebratory) within the lives of the depicted characters. All else stops and then continues. For the external reader or listener, there is time for delay since it is the process of telling the poem that is enjoyable; for the reader, as for the fictional audience within the poem, there is no rush to pick up the narrative thread and follow it to a conclusion.

Even within the narrative structure of the poem, though, there is one story that is not bound between events of the fictional present. The story of Scyld is situated at *Beowulf*'s opening limit, extending the poem's temporal setting and framing the story of Beowulf within legendary history. This story is not contextualized by being attributed to a "scop" who relates it on a particular occasion; it simply flows into the "main" narrative of *Beowulf*. The poem is not constructed, then, so that one time period—the narrative present—clearly predominates and controls, by containing, all other periods. Imaginatively, each of the stories (and other "digressions") opens up the temporal setting of the poem, framing it with references to the past (e.g., the story of creation, Cain's crime, and the lives of Heremod and Hildeburh) and the future (e.g., the burning of Heorot and the failure of the marriage between Freawaru and Ingeld to maintain peace). At the very moment when the reader becomes absorbed within the special isolated interval of the story's telling, she or he also imagines times beyond the limits of the poem's present. Two time periods—one encased within a very specific moment and one reaching out to embrace past or future, one framed and one framing—coincide in the stories. The frequency of these temporal pauses and escapes creates for the poem a time frame that is fluid; the narrative of Beowulf's life is not bound to the fictional present nor constrained by an urgency to advance the narrative.

Derrida, in speaking about the problem of locating a text's frame, refers specifically to Kant's third *Critique*—a text that is itself concerned with the "parergon"—but he also draws into question the whole notion of reading conceptual frames:

> I do not know what is essential and what is accessory in a work. . . .
> Where does the frame take place. Does it take place. Where does it begin.
> Where does it end. What is its internal limit. Its external limit. And its
> surface between the two limits.[50]

Reading *Beowulf* provokes—or should provoke—the same kinds of questions. The problem of the "digressions" has troubled many scholars and can be valued as a way to begin exploring the structural composition of the poem. To reconsider the implications of the term *digression* is to raise the question of what determines the center and the periphery of the poem. Frames are a way of shaping interpretation; sometimes they are suggested by the text, but often they are created by the reader as a way of organizing conceptions. Even those frames suggested by the text are not fixed objects. "There is," writes Derrida, "no natural frame" (81); the frame is "like wood. It creaks and cracks, breaks down and dislocates even as it cooperates in the production of the product, overflows it and is deduc(t)ed from it" (75). As readers, we set up frames and then shift them. Although we cannot read without a framework—a frame of reference, a set of assumptions, an understanding of some elements of the text as creating contexts for others—the structure is not absolute. It is to be expected that in an introduction to the poem, Klaeber would sort out for the reader the intrinsic from the extrinsic (doing in advance the reader's work of framing), but in fact, there is nothing in the poem to establish the location of primary meaning, and *Beowulf*, like other Anglo-Saxon art, is elaborately structured by frames that are fluid, playful, and left up to the reader's interpretation. The center and the periphery are relative and changeable.

Significant Repetition

The framing devices that I have described in *The Dream of the Rood*, *Daniel*, and *Beowulf* construct narrative divisions. Another type of frame is formed by the repetition of words or ideas. The narrative frame that surrounds *Beowulf*'s Finn episode is illustrative of a verbal repetition that sets off a passage of poetry as a distinct unit. (Frequently, frames formed by repetition coincide with the narrative frames that mark off a story within the story.) The lines immediately following the story of Finn contain several verbal echoes of the lines immediately preceding it: "gid" in line 1065 is repeated in 1160; "healgamen" in line 1066 is echoed by "gamen" in 1160; "sweg" (1063) and "medobence" (1067) are combined in line 1161 as "bencsweg"; and "sang" in line 1063 is paralleled by "asungen" in 1159. Adeline Bartlett described, composed lists of, and interpreted the function of this type of repetition.[51] These frames, or "envelope patterns," do delineate passages of poetry; like the narrative frames, however, the boundaries they suggest can be difficult to interpret, and can complicate rather than direct the interpretation of the poem. The Finn episode, although circumscribed by a pattern of verbal repetition, is (as I have argued) not complete and contained within its border.

Words or ideas can be repeated to indicate the beginning and end of a descriptive, as well as a narrative, passage. Sometimes a whole poem is framed by verbal or conceptual repetition. The riddles of the Exeter Book often have such frames; since the meaning—the solution—is not usually explicitly provided in the riddle, these poems are not as complete semantically (as self-contained) as the repetition would suggest. Completion, like the filling in of narrative gaps in an allusive story, depends on the interpretive work of the reader. The final verse of the "Bookmoth" riddle (47) echoes an idea, or image, described in the first verse:

> Moððe word fræt. Me þæt þuhte
> wrætlicu wyrd, þa ic þæt wundor gefrægn,
> þæt se wyrm forswealg wera gied sumes,
> þeof in þystro, þrymfæstne cwide
> ond þæs strangan staþol. Stælgiest ne wæs
> wihte þy gleawra, þe he þam wordum swealg.[52]

This is an unusual riddle in that its "solution"—the identification of the creature and of its strange behavior—is given and, in fact, frames the poem. The meaning of this riddle, then, would seem to be "sealed"; however, despite the frame, as Marie Nelson observes, "completion . . . is denied when the expected effect of eating words is denied; the moððe does not get any wiser."[53] Through its play with double meanings, the riddle juxtaposes the images of a worm eating the material of a book, and a reader consuming its knowledge, devouring its meaning; although the creature (which is sometimes described in human terms—"thief" or "guest") absorbs the text, it does not achieve the goal of that activity. So while the repetition in the final half-line signifies the completion of the poem, the action described within the frame is futile, ongoing, and difficult to comprehend. The "ambiguities"[54] within the language of the poem contradict and exceed the simplicity of the frame's statement. A limit of meaning is suggested and then played with.

The Framed Condition of Self-Referential Language

When words in the "Bookmoth Riddle" have a double significance, so that language becomes an object of attention, the poem displays a third kind of framing device. My observation that Old English poetic language frames itself through self-reference derives but differs from Bakhtin's description of "novelistic discourse" in *The Dialogic Imagination*. He says that such discourse "not only represents, but itself serves as the object of representation. Novelistic discourse is always criticising itself."[55] Through its self-criticism, this language places itself "in a framed condition," it becomes "bounded" (50).[56] It is not a "language" that pretends to convey meaning simply, while itself remaining transparent.[57]

For Bakhtin, the languages constituting a novel become delimited objects when they are perceived as existing within a network, or "system," of other languages. "Language," in this theory, refers to what would conventionally be called a "voice," having its source in a specific ideology and reflecting a particular point of view. The system of languages in a novel is complex; each of the intersecting languages carries with it traces of what has already been said regarding the object of its description. Novelistic discourse cannot exist outside of this context.[58] Poetry, on the other hand, is always removed from any social or ideological setting. According to Bakhtin, in "the poetic image," "the word forgets that its object has its own history of contradictory acts of verbal recognition, as well as that heteroglossia that is always present in such acts of recognition" (278). The poet, being in complete control of a language that is his obedient servant,

> is not able to oppose his own poetic consciousness, his own intentions to the language that he uses, for he is completely within it and therefore cannot turn it into an object to be perceived, reflected upon or related to. Language is present to him only from inside, in the work it does to effect its intention, and not from the outside, in its objective specificity and boundedness. (286)

My application of Bakhtin's description of novelistic discourse to poetry is a departure from his categorization of modes of literary language, a

categorization that severely limits possibilities of meaning and interpretation in any type of text other than the novel. He does modify his distinction by referring to "the *majority* of poetic genres" (264) and "the poetic
image *narrowly* conceived" (278; emphasis added), but his theory is structured upon a clear difference between the poem and the novel that allows
the novel a complexity of discourse denied the poem. Old English poetic
language, recorded at a time when several cultures intersected, represents
a convergence of world views (comparable to early Latin literature, which
Bakhtin describes as "[viewing] itself in light of the Greek word, through
the eyes of the Greek word" [61]).[59] This literature is "dialogized" and "het-
eroglossic"; it consists of more than one language, each one framed by its
difference from the others with which it participates.

Besides casting itself within a system of languages, a language can
refer to itself—represent itself as a contoured object—in other ways. Old
English poetry is very language-focused. Reading this poetry, making its
meaning, involves reflecting on words—their sounds, the patterns they
form (such as Bartlett's envelope pattern), their appearance on the page
(Cynewulf's runic signatures), and their double meanings. In the "Book-
moth" riddle (as Robinson has argued), "swealg" can mean both "to swallow" and "to take into the mind," "staþol" could be a "foundation" in the
sense of a manuscript page or a "foundation of thought," and "cwide"
could refer to a "sentence" or to something that is chewed. The two meanings of the poem intersect in its language, and the effect of the wordplay—
to describe the word as something that is both conceptual and ink on the
page—emphasizes the concreteness, the materiality, of language. The
method of the poem—the way it focuses the reader's attention on words—
and its meaning—that language has substance and texture—both describe
words as objects with limitations.

Often, the semantic possibilities of a word are limited by its context so
that the act of determining meaning is simplified. Robinson speaks of a
type of wordplay that allows two meanings of a word to coincide, with the
result that the poem becomes a subtle extended metaphor. In her article
"Some Uses of Paronomasia in Old English Scriptural Verse," Roberta
Frank describes wordplay that brings together the meanings of two or
more words through the resemblance of their sounds.[60] In the poem *Genesis*, "word" and "wyrd," associated aurally, are understood also to share a
common significance—God's "word" is "fate" (214); "Adam" and "eorðe"
are linked in *Genesis B* in a way that suggests Adam's connection to the
earth—his place of "origin" and his "matrix"—before his fall (217).

The aural relationship between words designates a conceptual connection that is necessary and laden with meaning. In Cynewulf's poems the
repeated association of "rod" and "rodor" "[implies] that the convergence

of heaven ["rodor"] and earth ["rod"] was predestined by God from the beginning, the link foreshadowed and made manifest in these two English words" (210–11). "Daniel" and "dom" are frequently heard in combination in the poem *Daniel*. Building on the Hebrew meaning of the name, the Old English words speak of Daniel's interpretations as "judgments," or readings of God's judgments, and "[show] how the prophet's name fore-shadowed his historical function, how events did but recapitulate sacred etymology" (216–17).

Paronomasia has been described as an "analogical relationship . . . between signifiers";[61] in Old English poetry, this association leads the reader to understand a corresponding analogy between signifieds. It is through this process, not through direct statement, that meaning is made. Words are not transparent media providing access to an already existing meaning, but objects whose particular characteristics have significance; meaning is constructed *in* words, not conveyed *through* them. During the process of interpretation, the reader stops to enjoy the rich potential of the medium. Paronomasia is a technique of composition—and is indicative of a way of reading—that places language "in a framed condition." Roberta Frank writes that paronomastic constructions can be "[arranged] so as to frame in a kind of envelope pattern particularly dramatic or elevated pas-sages" (225). The two songs in *Daniel* are examples of this construction. An elaborate frame results, comparable to the ornate border of a manu-script illumination. While the detail within the frame itself attracts and holds attention (because of its wordplay or its interlace), the reader is also aware that it contains and delimits a passage of poetry (or an image) that is meant to be seen as distinct. Like the dialogic language of Bakhtin's novels, Old English poetic language becomes "bounded" when it refers to itself; one mode of its self-reference is its focus on words and their inter-relationships.

Old English poetry also casts itself as something to be looked at when, through interjections and interpretations contained in the text, it speaks "about" itself. Such comments are common in *Beowulf*. They can be inserted into the story of Beowulf's adventures—"þæt wæs god cyning" (2390b), "Swa sceal mæg don" (2166b), "Hyrde ic þæt" (62a, 2163a, and 2172a)—or into a story within this larger narrative. The account of Modthryth's wickedness is punctuated by two observations: "Ne bið swylc cwenlic þeaw / idese to efnanne, þeah ðe hio ænlicu sy . . ." ("Such is not a queenly custom for a lady to perform, although she be unique . . . ," 1941b–42); "ealodrincende oðer sædan . . ." ("aledrinkers said otherwise . . . ," 1945).

In *The Dream of the Rood*, the dreamer and the cross refer to their own presence as perceivers and shapers of the story with such comments as "þuhte me þæt ic gesawe" (4), "geseah ic" (14b, 21b, 33b, 51b), "ic . . . ongytan meahte" (18), "þæt wæs God ælmihtig" (39b), and "ic þæt eall beheold" (58b). When the cross speaks of its present condition while giving an historical account—"on me syndon þa dolg gesiene" (46b)—it again draws attention to itself as the source of the narrative. The effect of such interjections is to "place" the text, preventing the reader from losing sight of its limitations. A narrative free from traces of its teller's presence appears to offer readers an infinite expanse to become absorbed by and to make their own; its borders are concealed. Old English poetry situates the reader at the edge of its stories where she or he shares the narrator's perceptions and interpretations.

Language is represented as something that has been shaped and that has limitations. In the novel, according to Bakhtin, language is perceived as limited in relation to other languages or points of view. Old English poetry, too, can be structured as a "dialogue" of "ideologies," but its boundedness, or opacity, does not depend upon this form. It is characteristic of Old English poetic language that it is not seen *through*, but is—and, I think, was—seen as something substantial (in sound and appearance) and thick with meanings. The poetic frame formed by techniques that draw attention to language (wordplay and commentary within the narrative) has a visual analogue in the borders of the illuminations of the Athelstan Psalter (fig. 13) and the Grimbald Gospels (fig. 15); like the animals who grasp and bite the edges of the image, and the angels who support the border's medallions, self-referential language looks back at the text from beyond its limits. Such borders were not uncommon in Anglo-Saxon illumination,[62] and the "tangibility" that they represent provides an image through which the opacity and texture of the contemporary poetry can be understood. Although this language is always "in a framed condition," the words are also always playing against their limits. The double meanings that focus the reader's attention on language also show meaning escaping delimitation, and paronomastic composition depends upon a word's signification increasing through its collocation with other words.

In Old English poetry and Anglo-Saxon art, frames frequently perform the function of tracing a limit, drawing attention to it, and then questioning it. Since frames (in general) are so "central" to the structure both of texts and of the reading process, the unusual function of Anglo-Saxon frames should be a key to understanding concepts specific to Anglo-Saxon reading. Meaning, it seems, was not perceived as being delineated and fixed, the goal to which interpretation was directed, but as something elusive, in process, and constructed by the reader through attention to language. The process of reading—lingering over the text's intricate design and complexity of meaning—seems to have been valued over reaching a moment when interpretation would be (imagined as) complete. Reading, in the sense of the transmission and interpretation of stories, often occurred in a social situation at times of celebration; it was a pleasurable activity and one that bound the community together. As indicated by framing structures, "raedan" did not mean to be directed toward an absorption in a meaning given within the poem or painting, but involved an enjoyment of the text's complexities and a questioning of its limits.

CHAPTER 3

Images of Storytelling:
The Presence of the Past in Old English Poetry

The copying of the four Old English poetic manuscripts occurred within a culture in which written language held a central place. The monastic reform of the second half of the tenth century had created a need for the transcription in England of continental manuscripts for liturgical use and for the establishment and enlargement of libraries. A renewed interest in scholarship and education was inspired by the reform. Æthelwold and his student Ælfric consciously developed English as a literary language.[1] In Æthelwold's biography it is recorded that he took great pleasure in explaining Latin books to his students in the English language, and in instructing them in grammar and meter.[2] Ælfric, besides writing extensive Old English prose, wrote his Latin Grammar in the belief that "stæfcræft is seo cæg ðe ðara boca andgiet unlycð" ("the craft of letters [grammatica] is the key that unlocks the understanding of books"). In his preface, he says that the Grammar should be useful to students of both Latin and Old English ("heo byð swa ðeah sum angyn to ægðrum gereorde," "it will be, however, an introduction to both languages").[3] Literacy was not limited to those who could read Latin; written texts could be transmitted in several ways. Some educated people who could not read Latin could read English, and texts would be read aloud to those who had not been taught to read either language. In this cultural context, Old English poetry was copied, bearing traces of oral composition and transmission, and reintroducing orality at the very moment of its transcription.[4]

Impressed by the oral qualities of the poetry and concerned with discovering the literature's sources, scholars have traditionally overlooked its tenth- or eleventh-century situation (or rather pretended to look through it, making it seem transparent).[5] Considering this to be only another stage in the literature's evolution, they have rushed to imagine the time and

89

place of its original, oral composition. This practice has been drawn into question through various persuasive arguments. Alain Renoir reasons:

> [Lacking] a convincing classification of all ancient and medieval poems according to the circumstances of their composition . . . many literary interpreters might do well to downgrade temporarily the importance of the actual circumstances of composition and to concentrate on these features which are typical of oral-formulaic rhetoric regardless of the circumstances in question.[6]

Allen Frantzen and Charles Venegoni argue that the search for origins is characteristic of Anglo-Saxon scholarship in general:

> The modes of inquiry it deploys are enabled by a myth or fiction of origins which allows the discourse to exist. Anglo-Saxon is a discipline in search of origins on many fronts which collectively represent what is oldest, earliest, primary in its cultural data: Ur-texts, the first uses of words, the earliest forms of dialects. These collective origins—a past which never existed—are analogous to a lost paradise, the recovery of which demands formation of a religion, or to a lost City of Gold, the search for which brings into being a mission of conquest. The assertion of mythic origins, in other words, necessitates and justifies the search for them. (143–44)[7]

The circularity and subjectivity of this supposedly empirical (i.e., logical and objective) method are apparent. The "desire for origins," which has come to dominate literary and historical studies, is an impulse particularly inappropriate for the study of Old English poetry—although the impulse is understandable, since the lack of "original" versions leaves a gap that is enticing to fill. I shall attempt to work outside this convention, adopting a theoretical perspective that draws into question evolutionary models and notions of distinct time periods arranged in a fixed chronological order.

The focus of this chapter will be the convergence of oral and written—past and present—represented in Old English poetry (especially that of the four poetic manuscripts). This topic necessarily concerns oral-formulaic traditions and transitional literacy—vast topics with extensive bibliographies. Although the implications of scholarship in these fields will be articulated throughout my discussion, I shall not attempt to repeat the work already done so well by others. Paul Zumthor offers a provocative definition of oral-formulaic structure, which hints at its implications for interpretation:

> [F]ormulaic style can be described as a narrative strategy: it inserts within the discourse, as it unfolds, lexical and syntactic rhythm se-

quences borrowed from other preexisting kinds of expression, thus referring the audience to a familiar semantic world.[8]

The subject of oral-formulaic composition and reception has been explored
in recent studies by Ruth Finnegan, John Miles Foley, Walter Ong, Jeff
Opland, Alain Renoir, Paul Zumthor, and others.[9] The concept of transitional literacy has been developed in several thought-provoking directions
by, among others, Franz Bäuml, Rosamund McKitterick, Katherine
O'Brien O'Keeffe, and Brian Stock.[10] Brian Stock speaks of the complex
coexistence of oral and written forms: "There is in fact no clear point of
transition from a nonliterate to a literate society. . . . The change . . . was
not so much from oral *to* written as from an earlier state, predominantly
oral, to various combinations of oral *and* written."[11] The two topics—oral-
formulaic composition and transitional literacy—are similarly interrelated
in complex ways; the difference between them is largely a matter of perspective. Existing scholarship has shown that certain characteristics of Old
English poetry are attributable to its production in a transitionally literate
society and its continuing dependence on structures of oral composition;
Old English poetry partakes, often self-consciously, of both oral and written traditions. My attempt to trace an appropriate hermeneutics will place
the poetry's oral-transitional character within a consideration of representations of nonlinear time.

Recollecting Words and Stories

The structural composition of the poetry indicates a conception of
time that was not linear. Several scenes of storytelling are represented in
Beowulf, one of which is well-known for its depiction of the process of oral
poetic composition.[12] On the day after Beowulf's defeat of Grendel, many
warriors followed the monster's tracks to his mere, the place of his death.
Returning to the hall they spoke of Beowulf's fame. Sometimes a king's
thane, a warrior laden with glory, mindful of tales ("gidda gemyndig,"
868b), one who remembered many old stories, found other words truly
bound ("word oþer fand / soðe gebunden," 871b–72a); a man often began
to recite skilfully the adventure of Beowulf, and to utter successfully an apt
story, to vary words ("wordum wrixlan," 874a).[13] The story of Beowulf is
constructed from other stories found in the memory of the teller, so that
the old and the new are joined together. By recasting other tales, the poet
shapes Beowulf's experience into a narrative.

Each grammatical unit of Old English poetic language—even the
word—is constructed, and each level of structural composition involves a

return and reference to what has already been said.[14] The Old English vocabulary itself was expanded mostly by building with linguistic materials already at hand, rather than by introducing loan words. New concepts, such as those developed to articulate aspects of Christianity, were framed in familiar words that must have carried with them traces of previous meanings.[15] Very few words were absolutely new in their denotation; prior concepts were never relegated absolutely to the past. In poetic composition, a word already in use could be recast in combination with another word to create a new word and concept. Words attested nowhere other than in *Beowulf* (perhaps having been created in the composition of that poem) include such compounds as "niht-bealu" ("night evil," 193), "sæ-meþe" ("sea weary," 325), and "eðel-wyn" ("native land joy," where either element could be the principal noun: "joy of native land" or "joyful native land," 2493 and 2885). The histories of the two words constructing the compound would converge so that past meanings would be renewed and altered in present language.[16]

Verbal repetition also occurs within individual poems; the two (or more) instances of the word may be identical in form, or they may differ, functioning as elements of compounds or as diverse parts of speech. James Rosier describes such repetition as "generative composition," since the first occurrence of a word generates a second (and sometimes a third) "within a few lines."[17] This process is a "habit of Old English composition" that provides "coherence" (193) and "continuity" (200). He attributes the continuity within the poetry to "the nature of the language itself" (202), and traces a relationship between the various types of verbal repetition I have described:

> The resource of and capacity for expanding and amplifying, for providing variety within, meaning through the lexicon in poetic composition, as for the cultivation of the lexicon in the language elsewhere (as in glosses, prose translation, etc.), is an in-turning process, a process of re-shaping, redistributing, indeed of recreating, by returning to the native stock and its formative models. (202)

Whenever a poet, or any Anglo-Saxon composer of language, returned to a word already in use and reshaped it to suit a new purpose, she or he would necessarily reintroduce all of that word's prior signification, explicit and implicit—all of the residue of its previous use. The present meaning would be the richer for this inclusion of the past.

The poet's work would have been like that of a "bricoleur." I take this concept from Claude Lévi-Strauss who says that the bricoleur, who is somewhat like a handyman,

is adept at performing a large number of diverse tasks. . . . His universe
of instruments is closed and the rules of his game are always to make do
with "whatever is at hand," that is to say with a set of tools and materials
which is always finite and is also heterogeneous because what it contains
bears no relation to the current project, or indeed to any particular project, but is the contingent result of all the occasions there have been to
renew or enrich the stock or to maintain it with the remains of previous
constructions or destructions. The set of the "bricoleur's" means . . . is to
be defined only by its potential use or, putting this another way and in
the language of the "bricoleur" himself, because the elements are collected or retained on the principle that "they may always come in handy."[18]

The bricoleur's "repertoire" is characterized by its heterogeneity, ex-
tensiveness, and limitation. His method is contrasted with that of an
engineer, whose "tools are conceived and procured for the purpose of the
project" (17). The difference between the two methods can be interpreted
as that between a survey looking toward the past and a plan projected
toward the future. What is achieved by the bricoleur depends upon what
he finds in his store of material; the result "will always be a compromise
between the structure of the instrumental set and that of the project" (21).
For the engineer, a desired end determines which materials and tools will
be collected as he attempts "to make his way out of and go beyond the
constraints imposed by a particular state of civilization" (19); as a result,
his completed project more closely resembles his initial purpose than does
that of the bricoleur. The bricoleur's work is routed through retrospection,
takes shape as it progresses, and is "limited by the particular history of
each piece and by those of its features which are already determined by the
use for which it was originally intended or the modifications it has undergone for other purposes" (19). While no two completed projects will ever
be identical, no one will ever be unique and original—its elements have
always been used before, they are always "second hand"—the "remains and
debris of events" (22).[19]

    Lévi-Strauss calls the bricoleur's store of materials and tools a "treas-
ury" (18). In Old English poetry, speech is frequently represented—probably self-reflexively on the part of the poet—as the unlocking of a verbal
storehouse (Andreas 316b and 601b, Beowulf 259b: "wordhoard onleac"
["unlocked his wordhoard"]; similarly, Andreas 470b: "wordlocan
onspeonn" ["unfastened his storehouse of words"]). The storehouse is hidden away inside the speaker; God's speech in Andreas is an unlocking of
his mind's treasure ("modhord onleac," 172b), in Juliana, Affricanus un-
fastens the enclosure of his soul when he responds to Eleusius ("ferðlocan
onspeon," 79b), and in Beowulf words are described as being released from
the speaker's breast ("Let ða of breostum . . . Weder-Geata leoð word ut

faran," 2550–51).[20] To speak is to draw on a reserve of words, a collection that is hidden away and protected like a precious object. Just as the bricoleur values his materials and keeps them for future use, the Anglo-Saxon poet and the speakers represented in the poems store words in their minds; words held in memory fill their treasure chests. When faced with a new project, the bricoleur surveys his collection, and the poet/speaker recollects words from a verbal repertoire. There is a limit to what is in the storehouse, and each tool or word is itself limited (and enriched) by the history of previous use that it bears.

The wordhoard does not only contain individual words. Fragments of verse are also material "at hand" for the poet, constituting a stock that has been developed through use. The process of composition would involve remembering a phrase appropriate, in some degree, to the present narrative or description, and reshaping it, altering a word or two but retaining its basic structure and meaning. The half-line "beorna beahgifa" describes King Æthelstan as a "ring-giver of warriors" in the opening of *The Battle of Brunanburh* (2a). Following the same grammatical structure (principal noun preceded by modifying genitive plural) and conveying a similar meaning, Christ is designated in *The Phoenix* as "weoruda wilgiefa" ("the hosts' giver of good," 465a), in *Christ II* as "eorla eadgiefa" ("happiness-giver of nobles," 546a), in *Andreas* as "engla eadgifa" ("happiness-giver of angels," 74a) and as "sawla symbelgifa" ("feast-giver of souls," 1417a), in *Elene* as "hæleða hyhtgifa" ("hope-giver of heroes," 851a), and in *Guthlac B* as "folca feorhgiefa" ("life-giver of people," 1239a).[21] All of these collocations are synonymous with "lord," perpetuating the myth of the secular leader's or deity's benevolence, and each involves the play of similarity and difference in the molding of that concept. There was no search for original, first-hand material; instead, what had already been used was used again and derived value through its repetition, versatility, and also through its acquired meanings.

Not only were verses recast to suit a new context; entire passages, concerning set themes, were also repeated formulaically.[22] Themes such as the "beasts of battle," the "exile," and the "hero on the beach" can be traced, and their transformations explored, throughout the poetry.[23] Their recurrence indicates that familiarity was sought; the "beasts of battle" passage in, for example, *The Battle of Brunanburh*, would have reflected and renewed depictions of carnage in stories previously told, binding the new to the old and drawing the past into the present. The poet's recollection and repetition of the theme would have signified continuity and the cyclic movement of time; Zumthor describes such poetic utterances as "spontaneously recursive."[24]

Lévi-Strauss, in his examination of the method of the bricoleur, traces a mode of mythic, scientific thought. Since his focus is on the collector/constructor (as representative of a way of thinking), my analogy has centred on the role of the poet. James Rosier's description of "generative composition" is also concerned only with the poet's activity. Reading (or listening to) the poetry, however, would have involved a similar process of retrospection, recollection, awareness of the past. Greenfield, Bonjour, and Renoir consider the associations made by the reader between different occurrences of a formulaic theme, and between their contexts.[25] Associations are also made between specific instances of a word or a formulaic half-line. The poet's work and that of the reader are not distinct. When the poet surveys words, verses, and themes hoarded in her or his memory and chooses the most appropriate material with which to build the new poem, she or he is interpreting that word (or verse, or theme) in light of its various contexts. The audience performs the same activity; familiar with the poet's repertoire of words, verses, and themes, they hear the echoes, simultaneously remembering the previous occurrences and listening to the present instance.[26] Hearing Christ described as "weoruda wilgiefa," the audience of *The Phoenix* recalls (not necessarily consciously) the portrayal of a secular ruler as "beorna beahgifa," and understands the Lord to be as generous as a king. Secular and sacred myth reinforce each other for their mutual benefit; concepts of the generosity of the gift-giving pagan ruler of the past are transferred through poetry to the Christian Lord presently being exalted.[27] With no expectation of hearing an original composition— "original" implying that what was composed in the past should be sealed off, kept distinct from the present composition—the audience witnesses the convergence of past and present.

The concept of the past as continuing into, and being apparent in, the present is consistent with the syntactic structure of Old English poetry. "Variation," like the formulaic patterning of linguistic units, creates meaning through the play of resemblance and difference. When an idea is restated in a new way, from a different perspective, at a later moment, it is reconceptualized by poet and reader. While formulaic verses and themes circle back through time intertextually, past concepts are made present within the context of an individual poem (usually within a discrete passage) through variation. A brief passage from *The Battle of Brunanburh* demonstrates this cyclic movement:

> siðþan sunne up
> on morgentid,   mære tungol,
> glad ofer grundas,   godes condel beorht,
> eces drihtnes . . .   (13b–16a)[28]

The passage flows from the subject ("sunne") to an adverb ("up") and an adverbial phrase ("on morgentid"), back to another subject ("mære tungol"), on to the verb ("glad") and an adverbial phrase ("ofer grundas"), back again to a subject ("godes condel beorht") which is accentuated by an adjectival phrase ("eces drihtnes"). Twice, there is a return to and rephrasing of the subject of the passage, with the result that the reader is provided with three parallel images of the sun. Metaphoric and literal description combine in the meeting of "sun," "glorious star," and "God's bright candle." The subject is not left behind as something that has already been expressed when the sentence moves "forward" to disclose its predicate, and no single description eventually replaces the others—they occur simultaneously.

The inflection frees the syntax so that words are not locked into a position according to their role in the sentence. Since the grammatical form of a word indicates its function, words and phrases can continually be added and can be understood as referring back to a description that has already been given. (Because "eces drihtnes" is in the genitive case, we know that it redescribes "godes"). Variation results in the accumulation of multiple layers of parallel description. Meaning is not final and complete; although something has already been said, it can always be said again, differently. Since texts do not only reflect but also create ways of perceiving, syntax can be understood as indicating and structuring notions of time; just as modern English syntax, in which each word or phrase has its place and moment, constructs our desire for chronology, Old English variation, allowing for movement between past and present, would have produced in its audience a nonlinear concept of time.

Interruption, Repetition, and Delay

Narrative progresses slowly in Old English poetry; there is time for repetition and delay. Since narrative is, in a most basic definition, a shaping of time through the ordering of depicted events, Anglo-Saxon concepts of time should be suggested by the narrative structure of Old English poetry. When Roland Barthes formulated his description of the "langue", or universal language, of narrative, he articulated issues of chronology and pacing.[29] "Cardinal functions"—the key moments that constitute the framework of the narrative—are read as being bound to each other by chronology and logic:

> Everything suggests, indeed, that the mainspring of narrative is precisely the confusion of consecution and consequence, what comes *after* being read in narrative as what is *caused by*; in which case narrative would be a systematic application of the logical fallacy denounced by Scholasticism

in the formula 'post hoc, ergo propter hoc'—a good motto for Destiny, of
which narrative all things considered is no more than the 'language'. (94)

Between these crucial moments, are "areas of rest," "deviations" which can
"lead astray," but which are included by the narrative within its language
(95 and 117). This elaborate ordering of time is a fiction of the narrative as
much as are the portrayed events: the chronology is the reader's assumption based on the consecution of events, and the pacing is almost always
pure invention.[30] "Real" time has little to do with narrative time, which is
shaped by the poet's and readers' perception and expectation of temporal
movement.

The pace of a narrative depends on the frequency and duration of
deviations in relation to cardinal moments—in Old English poetry, there
is a high proportion of deviations. These can be digressions of either a
narrative or descriptive nature, or variations enhancing a previous depiction. Both are elaborations, working out in detail and ornamenting the
essentials of the narrative.[31] Inserted into the unfolding story, they entice
the reader to delay, to pause and enjoy the decoration they offer. While the
narrative, representing a series of events, advances toward its close, the
elaborations, creating a design that deviates from direct representation,
make little or no progress. Exaggerating the difference, it can be said that
the individual narrative moment, or "cardinal function," has an end outside itself, while each elaboration is an end in itself.

An analogy to Old English narrative structure can be found in Anglo-
Saxon manuscript illumination. If those aspects of the painting that
advance a "primary" signification are compared to a narrative's "cardinal
moments," and those that provide decoration to deviations away from a
story, we see in the manuscript art the circuitous structure of the poetry.
The Chi Rho page of the Book of Kells (produced ca. 800, probably at Iona)
is decorated with an abundance of pattern and imagery that almost over-
whelms the initials of Christ's name (fig. 16). The reader's recognition of
the signification of the painting is delayed by the elaborate design, and
once the letters have been deciphered, there is a desire to return again to
the web of decoration. Although it has been argued by Suzanne Lewis that
each element of the decorative imagery—human heads, an otter, fish,
cats, mice, and butterflies—supports (offers a route to) the significance of
the Chi Rho, it is equally possible (and, arguably, more appropriate) to
enjoy the imagery for its own sake.[32] There is a temptation to follow the
lines that lead nowhere except into knots and spirals; time can be spent
disentangling the figures embedded in the labyrinthine design.

Even in the late tenth century, when, in art as in literature, there was
an increased exchange of concepts and styles between England and the

16. Chi Rho monogram. Trinity College Dublin MS 58, fol. 34r.

continent, and Anglo-Saxon painting became more representational, ornament continued to interrupt narrative signification. In the Benedictional
of St. Æthelwold, twenty-eight illuminations depict choirs, saints, and biblical scenes.[33] The manuscript, however, is as remarkable for its ornamentation as for its abundance of representation. The miniature illuminating

the blessing for Palm Sunday depicts Christ's entry into Jerusalem (fig. 17). Its narrative has as "cardinal" features the figures of Christ and the apostles approaching the city of worshippers. The reader's attention is lead astray by the ornamental frame and also by decorative details of the representational figures—the lines of the draperies and the colors and textures of the buildings. Interlace and spiral patterns have been replaced by acanthus and swirling lines, but in their profusion of ornament the Benedictional drawings repeat the narrative structure of the Chi Rho page. Figures

17. Entry into Jerusalem. London British Museum, Add. MS 49598, fol. 45v.

are obscured by boughs and buildings as they were by the linear patterns of the earlier illumination. The proportion of deviation in relation to linear narrative progress creates a temporal rhythm that allows for delay.

Klaeber has described the narrative structure of *Beowulf* as being characterized by a "lack of steady advance"; "the author," he says, "has contrived to expand the narrative considerably in the leisurely epic fashion."[34] Besides raising the question of which narrative and descriptive elements are central and which are peripheral,[35] the *Beowulf* "digressions" affect the pacing of the poem and its representation of time. Lines 64 to 114 are structured according to a continual movement away from and back to the narrative path. Hrothgar's success as a ruler and his building of Heorot (64–82a) constitute what Barthes would describe as "hinge-points of the narrative" (93). In a deviation that defies notions of chronology and suspense (typically the impulses of narrative), the poem refers forward to a fire and feud occurring in a future beyond its scope (82b–85). Returning to the present and introducing a principal character, the poem describes the suffering of a powerful demon at hearing the festivities within the hall (86–90a). *Beowulf* strays again from its narrative path when the topic of one of the songs overheard by the demon is related in detail (90b–98); this deviation is both concurrent with the "main" story— in that it is contained within a song presently being sung—and (extremely) previous to it—since the subject of the song is Creation. In the next few lines, the two topics that have followed the course of the narrative coincide: the joy of the warriors is linked to an identification of Grendel and a description of his evil deeds (99–104a). In another movement back to the distant, biblical past, the poem turns to the story of Grendel's lineage, tracing his ancestry back to Cain (104b–114).

The building of Heorot, the celebrations of the Danes, Grendel's suffering and evil-doing are as bound to each other (and to previous and subsequent "cardinal" events) as are the "hinge-points" of James Bond novels as described by Barthes ("the telephone rang. . . . Bond answered", "Bond's future partner offers him a light from his lighter . . . Bond refuses"): each event is read as "coming to fruition" in the next. The spaces between these moments, however, are decorated with the details of past and future events to such an extent that the decoration exceeds the "essentials" of the story. Comprehension of the story, like the deciphering of the letters of the Chi Rho, is hindered and delayed by the elaborations, and the time spent telling or hearing the poem is luxuriously extended as the narrative jumps forward and circles back. The consecution of the cardinal events does lead to the interpretation that they are consequential (the festivities of the Danish warriors are a result of Heorot having been built) and, therefore, chronological (the cause precedes the result), but the narrative thread is difficult to follow; Anglo-Saxon narrative seems not to have been primarily concerned with the representation of chronology. The passage from *The Battle of Brunanburh* that has served as an example of variation explicitly describes a duration of time, contributing to the temporal structure of the poem. Variation, like digressions, however, delays the unfolding of a story, so that the production of the narrative thread in *Brunanburh* is repeatedly interrupted. The narrative function of the passage requires only the delineation of the time of the battle—from sunrise till sunset ("siðþan sunne upp . . . glad . . . oð [heo] . . . sag to setle," 13b–17a). All other descriptions—variations restating the subject or modifying the verb—are deviations delaying and complicating the representation of chronology. "Narrative," says Barthes, is the "language of Destiny" (94), because it signifies consequence through its depiction of consecutive events; a linguistic unit becomes confused with a temporal one. The sentence from *Brunanburh* represents a day, and its circuitous structure indicates a conception of time as other than linear progression.

Images of Storytelling

The predominance of "deviations" in Anglo-Saxon narrative is another trace of the oral in the written. An orally related story tends to allow for repetition and elaboration; its spontaneity produces a fluid structure. Storyteller and listener can become distracted by "unessential" details of the narrative; the elaboration of a story, like the fascinating designs of a manuscript page, can absorb the reader's attention, so that the progression of events seems unimportant. Writing tends to control a narrative; events and descriptions are inscribed in a most appropriate order, and repetition is corrected. The orally told story has no spatial limitations, but the written narrative is organized on the page, its words lined up from left to right. There are probably no texts that display either of the two modes of transmission in such an extreme state; in Old English poetry, oral and written merge. The representation of time in written narrative would continue to be shaped by conceptions of time produced through oral storytelling.[36]

The compositional structure of Old English poetry, then, speaks of a concept of time that was not bound by chronology, and says that the representation of the past in tenth- and eleventh-century poetry can be read not as a reference to a previous storytelling situation, complete within its own time frame, but as the coincidence of the oral and (or in) the written. Encountering traces of the oral in the written—structures such as formulaic verses and variation, as well as depictions of storytelling—the present-day reader sees the overlap, the merging together, of two cultures. Rather than trying to distinguish the two (identifying the one as the source for the other), the overlap can be studied as one would study the layers of images that accumulate to form a cavepainting. To do so is to resist chronological ordering, to read "backward" through the written to the oral, instead of constructing a genealogy wherein the written poem descends from an (always hypothetical) oral ancestor. The analogy with cave art suggests that the two forms of poetry are not separable but that each takes meaning from the other.

In the previous chapter, I considered Whitney Davis's analysis of the construction of image and nonimage in paleolithic cave art. The methodology that he uses in that study[37] provides a model for reading the images of storytelling that underlie written Old English poetry. Davis examines palimpsests that consist of "early" nonimage elements that have deliberately been taken into "later" images, so that sometimes "two or more images may depend upon a single shared line" (131). He says that, "A meaningful representation does not always and only derive from, replicate, and vary a ground of absolutely meaningless stuff (lumps, marks, sound waves), but also derives from, replicates, and varies a ground with other meanings" (133), and goes on to conjecture that "the artist ultimately takes control of what is initially presented simply as an inherent and necessary fact of making marks" (135). In the art he is studying, lines were formed by engravers who used their fingers to gouge through soft clay, or a tool to incise a hard surface. The artist, Davis says, "could not easily change or erase his work. We can therefore watch a chain of replications piling up as an enormous palimpsest of variants" (125). As I have argued in chapter 2, Davis's interpretation of the alteration of cave drawings as a progression, over time, away from errors of perception and toward recognizable images is in keeping with conventional concepts of evolution. His observations on (what I am calling) the "presence of the past" suggest a nonlinear concept of history, but an evolutionary model is conjured again when he describes the later images as an improvement upon those that came earlier. Nevertheless, the cave art that Davis describes provides an image of the past, and of its reuse, which is helpful in understanding the temporal implications of Old English poetic structure.

The wall is never blank, and what the artist finds there already has meaning; this meaning, like the lines themselves, is inevitably taken into the new image. The inscription from the past cannot be ignored or bracketed off, nor are its methods and meanings distinct from those of the present drawing. Just as lines engraved in the past are part of the ground on which the painting takes shape, modes and situations of previous oral storytelling would have been held in the memory of the Anglo-Saxon writer of poetry, and would have been worked into the new design. The written record—one way of remembering—recalls another; a memory of storytelling inspires a narrative which, in turn, evokes a memory. Accounts of the relating of tales in *Beowulf* explicitly describe situations of storytelling; although *The Wanderer* does not announce that it is depicting a festive gathering in which a story was told, it represents an immediate expression of thought and experience. In a late tenth-century literary environment, such texts provide, (with)in writing, images of storytelling; they reintroduce circumstances of oral transmission in which a member of a community would relate a tale or an experience at a social gathering. As the speaker casts her- or himself as "I," whether in writing or reading aloud from the manuscript page, a fiction is constructed. A reciprocal role as the audience of an oral poem is adopted by the readers or listeners. The image of storytelling—recognized by its readers as having been "drawn" in the past, but also as having significance in the present—perpetuates a mode of reading.

Bede's account of Cædmon's poetic composition provides a graphic illustration of the intersection of oral and written modes, as well as of the coincidence of two languages and two cultures.[38] Katherine O'Brien O'Keeffe has studied transcriptions of *Cædmon's Hymn*, a poem that (unusual for Old English poetry) exists in fourteen Anglo-Saxon manuscripts spanning several centuries.[39] In the earliest (eighth-century) manuscripts, the poem is recorded in the Northumbrian dialect as a gloss to the Latin *Historia ecclesiastica*.[40] No Latin copies survive from the ninth or tenth century, and not all of those from the eleventh and twelfth centuries include the Old English *Hymn*; in those that do, it has been copied into the margin. The five surviving copies of the Alfredian translation of Bede's *History* (all written in the tenth and eleventh centuries) contain the *Hymn* in its West Saxon form within the main text. Comparing methods of transcription, Katherine O'Brien O'Keeffe finds that, although the text of the poem as a gloss in the eleventh-century Latin manuscripts is "extremely stable" (15), the poem as copied in contemporary West Saxon manuscripts shows "extensive variation" (15).[41] She interprets the variance as indicating "a fluid transmission of the *Hymn* somewhere between the formula-defined process which is an oral poem and the graph-bound object which is a text" (15); the scribe, although working within a tradition of writing that would act as "a very powerful constraint on variance," was writing in a vernacular, "living" language, and would continue to choose between possible formulae in the composition of the text (15–16). Like the poet composing orally, the writer would remember set phrases, choose from them, and adjust them according to her or his present semantic, alliterative, and rhythmic requirements.

Cædmon's Hymn did not change into a stable written text at the moment of its inscription, leaving its oral history behind. O'Keeffe's study of the poem's manuscript transmission illustrates the overlapping of the two modes for both the writer and the reader. The scribe would have been involved simultaneously in the activities of reading (the poem he or she was copying) and composing (the poem as reproduced). Her or his transcription records that the text was not perceived as fixed; the words already there (the lines on the wall) did not have to be preserved, unchanged, or relegated absolutely to the past but could be shaped by the present act of writing.[42] The audience for the late Anglo-Saxon poem, like someone gazing upon a cavepainting, would see a double image. Whether this audience were reading the poem from the manuscript page or hearing it read aloud, they would reexperience the situation and process of listening to an orally composed poem.

In the narrative of Bede's account of Cædmon, oral and written modes are represented as opposites, each belonging to its own domain. As the story proceeds, Cædmon's spontaneous, formulaic verse is assimilated into the learned, monastic tradition. The illiterate cowherd must learn of the scriptures ("godcunde stafas" ["divine letters"]) before he composes, and while he recites the poems, his teachers ("lareowas," also described as "boceras" ["scribes"]) record them. Bede's text would seem to repeat the work of the scribes—transforming the oral into the written—and then to take the transformation a step further by placing the fixed text within a narrative frame. Although the story speaks of the mastery of the oral by the written, and the fact of the poem's transcription apparently attests to this, the manuscript history of *Cædmon's Hymn* says otherwise. The mode and situation of oral storytelling are, in fact, perpetuated by Bede's written description of them, and the variation seen in the manuscript versions records a convergence, a survival of the fluidity of oral composition and interpretation in a written text. Two ways of remembering are also recorded in tenth- and eleventh-century West Saxon copies of the story of Cædmon: while the text is remembered precisely because it is written, the poem also inspires formulaic memory, which recalls potential phrases and allows for change.[43] What is represented as a simple opposition is, on an interpretive level, a complex interaction of narrative traditions.

Two languages, representing two cultures, also appear in the narrative to belong to distinct realms, but like the two compositional modes, they meet in its transmission. Allen Frantzen begins his deconstruction of the *Hymn* by describing our conventional reading:

> We see that once the voice mute in secular song can speak, it speaks in the new tongue of the new religion—for Bede gives us a perfect dichot-

omy of its institutionalized discourse, the native hall, with the harp at the feast—and opposite it the learned monastic songfest of holy worship.[44]

In order for Cædmon's English songs to be meaningful to Bede and his audience, they must be informed by the Latin tradition; a translator mediates between the two worlds, providing Cædmon with suitable subject matter. Although within the fiction Cædmon composes his songs in English, Bede writes in a monastic setting for a Christian audience and translates the *Hymn* into Latin. In the initial act of recording the story, Cædmon's language is appropriated by Latin, just as the cowherd/poet is appropriated by the Church. English, however, inscribes itself in the margin of even the earliest copies of the *Historia ecclesiastica*. The two languages carry on a dialogue throughout the manuscript history (Latin may translate English, English may gloss or translate Latin) never presenting a unified voice and never speaking without a recognition of the other's presence. The Latin narrative composed by Bede is a response to the unrecorded English poem; it describes the origin of Cædmon's hymn and directs the reader in interpreting its significance. The Old English gloss written in the margin is, in turn, a response to the story about it. The gloss makes the narrative's reference concrete and insists that the poem not be fully recuperated by "the new tongue of the new religion"; it addresses an audience—perhaps not identical to the audience of Bede's Latin *History*—who would read the Old English (or hear it read) and want it preserved.[45] The Alfredian translation and its copies again speak to an audience literate in Old English, responding to (and thereby creating) the continuing significance of both the poem and its narrative frame.[46]

An essential distinction between the two interacting languages is recognized by Bede and Bakhtin. Bede follows his Latin paraphrase of the *Hymn* with the apology: "Hic est sensus, non autem ordo ipse verborum, quae dormiens ille canebat; neque enim possunt carmina, quamvis optime conposita, ex alia in aliam linguam ad verbum sine detrimento sui decoris ac dignitatis transferri" ("This is the sense, but not the exact order, of the words which he sang while sleeping; for songs cannot, however well composed, be translated word for word from one language to another without some loss of beauty & dignity"). The Latin paraphrase of *Cædmon's Hymn* differs from the Old English, not only in avoiding a literal translation, but in its meter, its layout on the manuscript page, and its punctuation. There is a common territory—"sensus"—where the languages meet (or there could be no translation, no dialogue), but each has its own particular characteristics—its "decor" and "dignitas"; one language cannot echo another, but will inevitably alter and enhance it, adding its own voice.

Bakhtin describes the intersection of two languages in a text as "a dialogue between points of view, each with its own concrete language that cannot be translated into the other."[47] Whenever Latin and Old English translate or gloss each other, two cultures, with distinct "world views" or "opinions,"[48] continue to speak in the text. This continuity of dialogue is in itself a survival of the oral. Even inscribed in a manuscript the story of Cædmon is not fixed and complete, but represents an ongoing colloquy. Bakhtin's hermeneutic centers around the importance of the response to the significance of speech (and therefore to the significance of a written text—in his view, the novel):

> In the actual life of speech, every concrete act of understanding is active: it assimilates the word to be understood into its own conceptual system filled with specific objects and emotional expressions, and is indissolubly merged with the response, with a motivated agreement or disagreement. To some extent, primacy belongs to the response, as the activating principle: it creates the ground for understanding. . . . Understanding comes to fruition only in the response. Understanding and response are dialectically merged and mutually condition each other; one is impossible without the other. (282)

Glosses and translations of Bede's story and *Cædmon's Hymn* are the traces of a reader's response, a response emanating from a specific cultural environment with its own "conceptual system." This response inserts another worldview into a position alongside of the one already represented, and creates an opening in the text for the responses of other readers. Readers see each language in light of the other; although (or because) the two have distinct identities in relation to each other, there is no simple opposition with one eventually subsuming the other, nor do the differences become muted so that the two are perceived as one.

The history of the story of Cædmon as a "written" text contradicts the apparent binary oppositions in the narrative; scribes, glossators, and translators—as readers—did not respond to the text as if it represented a progression away from oral vernacular and toward written Latin language. The language and compositional mode of the past are remembered and have relevance when reintroduced later in the transmission of the story. When eleventh-century scribes, writing in a culture of great literary production, draw from remembered, potential half-lines (rather than from the texts they are copying), they allow a voice from the past to speak. The languages that merge to form the "heteroglossy" of the story of Cædmon include voices from past and present, as well as voices from different cultural environments.

Distinct characteristics are attributed to reading from a written text as opposed to listening to the relating of a story. Both the reading processes and their settings are thought to be different. While the reader of a written text confronts a complete and unchangeable work, whose author is absent and time of composition distant, the person who hears a story related can interrupt its telling to effect change, since its author is present and its composition ongoing. The different implications of the two modes, from a compositional point of view, are poetically evoked by Gabrielle Roy in her novel *The Road Past Altamont*.[49] Christine's mother creates her stories continually, spontaneously, with her audience gathered around her:

> The old theme of my grandparents' arrival in the west had been to my mother a sort of canvas on which she had worked all her life as one works at a tapestry, tying threads and commenting upon events like fate, so that the story varied, enlarged, and became more complex as the narrator gained age and perspective. Now when my mother related it again, I could scarcely recognize the lovely story of times past that had so enchanted my childhood; the characters were the same, the route was the same, and yet nothing else was as it used to be.
>
> Sometimes we interrupted her.
>
> "But that detail didn't appear in your first versions. That detail is new," we said with a hint of resentment perhaps, so anxious were we, I imagine, that the past at least should remain immutable. For if it too began to change . . .
>
> "But it changes precisely as we ourselves change," said Maman (123)

Christine herself writes her stories, and becomes alienated from the objects of her description:

> How well do I remember that year of my life, the last perhaps when I lived quite close to people and things, not yet somewhat withdrawn, as happens inevitably when one yields to the intention to set things down in words. . . . I remained for some time at ease in life . . . not slightly to one side. Seldom since then have I been able to return completely to this or to see things and human beings otherwise than through words, once I had learned to use them as fragile bridges for exploration . . . and, it is true, sometimes for communication also. I became by degrees a sort of watcher over thoughts and human beings. . . . (133)

Oral storytelling situations and structures, though, are restaged through written Old English poetry. The inscribed texts, rather than becoming objects detached from their producers and unalterable by their readers, remain open and variable, reinvoking the subjectivity of the composer and the reader. If the poem were read aloud to a listening audience, the performer would act the part of the producer, introducing that person's presence to the reading situation. The reader of late Old English prose is frequently addressed as "one who reads that or hears it read" ("se ðe ðæt ræde, oþþe rædan gehyre"). Whether the manuscript poem were read privately by an individual or heard through oral presentation, the reader would witness its process of composition; phrases added in variation would indicate that a rewriting, a redescribing, was constantly occurring. Poetry, a medium for remembering in times before written texts, continues to recollect both the stories and the way they were told and received.

The Substance of the Written Text

The written poetry exists at and creates the juncture of two forms of composition and reading, where spontaneity encounters preconception, temporality, permanence, and hearing is sometimes replaced by seeing; but it also blurs these distinctions. Although it is inevitable that the past will be present (the wall is never blank), several poems express a self-conscious awareness of the convergence, and the paradox that it creates. The "Reed Pen" riddle in the Exeter Book is one example:

Ic wæs be sonde,	sæwealle neah,
æt merefaroþe,	minum gewunade
frumstaþole fæst;	fea ænig wæs
monna cynnes,	þæt minne þær
on anæde eard beheolde,	
ac mec uhtna gehwam	yð sio brune
lagufæðme beleolc.	Lyt ic wende
þæt ic ær oþþe sið	æfre sceolde
ofer meodubence	muðleas sprecan,
wordum wrixlan.	Þæt is wundres dæl,
on sefan searolic	þam þe swylc ne conn,
hu mec seaxes ord	ond seo swiþre hond,
eorles ingeþonc	ond ord somod,
þingum geþydan,	þæt ic wiþ þe sceolde
for unc anum twam	ærendspræce
abeodan bealdlice,	swa hit beorna ma
uncre wordcwidas	widdor ne mænden.[50]

This riddle can be solved by the reader who can answer the question "what communicates by silent speech?" or "what transforms the oral into the written?" Following the logic of an Old English riddle involves adopting an inquisitive stance, making what might have come to seem unremarkable through familiarity into "something of a wonder." In the "Reed Pen" riddle, speaking and writing are seen to be the same, in that they are both social acts through which communication occurs, and also different, since they require distinct media and reach different audiences. The poem describes the act of writing, but always in comparison to that of speaking: the instrument of writing is mouthless, unlike a speaker, but it performs its function at the mead bench, taking the place of oral speech. The unique characteristics of writing (it is a preconceived inscription—the pen is pressed ["geþydan"] by someone's intention ["ingeþonc"]) and silent reading (it is intimate ["for unc anum twam"] and private ["beorna ma / uncre wordcwidas widdor ne mænden"]) are viewed with curiosity.

In her article "The Paradox of Silent Speech in the Exeter Book Riddles," Marie Nelson says that the riddle objects "exploit paradox" by denying that they can speak at the very moment when they tell us about themselves.[51] But she understates the complexities of the contradictions. The riddle objects to which she refers—an engraved chalice (riddle No. 48) as well as the reed pen—cannot "really" utter a sound but are presented in the poems as speaking, but also as telling us that their speech is silent, which is true because it is written in a manuscript. But if the poem were then to be read aloud, the speaker would be posing as an object that was telling us of its silent speech thereby adding further contradictory statements about the mode of the text's transmission. The different layers and kinds of textuality that have accumulated at this transitional literary moment are regarded with amazement through riddles like the "Reed Pen."

While the phenomenon that attracts interest in the "Reed Pen" riddle is the transmission of a written text, the "Bookmoth" riddle is concerned with a manuscript's reception.[52] Both poems describe a written textual environment against a backdrop—explicit or suggested—of an oral one. Just as the specific characteristics of writing are the focus of the "Reed Pen" riddle, in the "Bookmoth" riddle, the materiality of the written text is accentuated. As Fred Robinson has shown, both the swallowing of food and the absorbing of knowledge are signified by the words "swealg," "staþol," and "cwide";[53] through this wordplay, wisdom is tentatively portrayed as being as substantial as parchment. The attitude of the poem is one of surprise at the way a book makes knowledge (which in an oral tradition could only be held in memory) tangible. Considering the manuscript's materiality, it is even more remarkable that its meaning lies beyond the page and is, ultimately, as intangible as that of speech—the swallower of the page gains no wisdom.[54]

The narrative of the poem *Daniel* is structured around acts of reading: the interpretation of Nebuchadnezzar's dreams, the two songs, and the

writing on the wall are the links that form the narrative. The reading of
Daniel is as demanding as the reading depicted in it. Wordplay "hints" at
meanings beyond the literal, significations that must be discovered, as
must the meanings of the mysteries of Nebuchadnezzar's dreams or the
angel's writing (each of which is described as "gerynu" [149, 746] or "run"
[541, 740]).[55] A listening audience would interpret clues offered in the
sounds of words; lacking this aural level of signification, a reader looking
at the text would have the advantage of being able to reread and spend
time discovering the clues. The external reader's work of deciphering the
poem is mirrored and revealed in the poem by Daniel's interpretations; he
explains the king's first dream ("sægde him wislice wereda gesceafte,"
160), interprets his second ("him witgode wyrda geþingu," 545), and reads
the writing on the wall ("he him bocstafas / arædde," 739–40).

In this poem that foregrounds reading, both oral and written "texts"
must be deciphered. Although the dreams are constituted primarily of images, and convey their meanings visually (verbs such as "ywan," "ætywan,"
"eowan" [each meaning "to show"], and "geseon" ["to see" or "look"] indicate the importance of sight), they are described as having a sound. The
first is introduced, "com on sefan hwurfan swefnes woma" ("the sound of a
dream came into his mind," 110), and after the second Nebuchadnezzar
"secgan ongan swefnes woman" ("began to explain the sound of the
dream," 538). In his edition of *Daniel*, Robert Farrell (following R. F. Leslie)
suggests that "woma" had undergone a "semantic shift" from "sound" to
"announcement," and that "'swefnes woma' is perhaps best taken as
'dream-vision' in all three instances in Daniel. . . ."[56] In a culture that
includes the oral transmission of texts, however, a dream could be represented as having a sound in that, like other messages, it would be heard,
interpreted, and understood. Farrell's translation may be more appropriate
to our own visually oriented culture than to the more oral one of Anglo-
Saxon England. When the dreams are told to Daniel, their interpreter,
they explicitly enter an oral tradition. Like the songs, they exist only in
memory and must be conveyed through an intermediary. The writing on
the wall has permanence; Daniel can stand before it. So while there are
similarities between the two types of texts in *Daniel*—both are messages
that can be learned from but only after a difficult interpretation has been
achieved—there are also differences. The verbs "secgan" ("to explain") and
"areccan" ("to relate") describe the interpretation of both the dreams and
the writing, but "araedan" ("to read" or "interpret") is used only to convey
Daniel's reading of the angel's message. The difference between oral and
written can be seen most clearly when the first dream is compared to the
writing on the wall: whereas the king cannot remember the details of his
dream, and having been lost from memory, the text must be reestablished,

the inscription is a substantial and permanent text, available for all to see. *Daniel* represents the reading of temporal and permanent, heard and seen texts, emphasizing the importance and complexity of interpretation.

Implications of an Ironic Stance

Adopting an ironic stance in relation to its own form or content is another way Old English poetry demonstrates a self-conscious awareness of its oral and written character. In his article "Varieties and Consequences of Medieval Literacy and Illiteracy,"[57] Franz Bäuml defines a perceptual difference that occurs during the transmission of a written text as opposed to an oral one:

> A further consequence both of the fixity and the independent existence of a fixed text is the fact that it does not necessarily require the commitment of its bearer to its content; the scribe, the reciter, or the reader of a written text can confront that text critically, even ironically. In short, not only in a physical sense is the distance greater between fixed text and writing author or reading reciter than between oral poem and oral poet, but also in a perceptual sense. (249–50)

Distance allows for irony, and irony "testif[ies] to a recognition of distance between author, narrator, text, and public, and to the narrative possibilities this distance offers" (253). The ironic stance arises from and creates an "alienation" or "defamiliarization" in the audience's response to the text. What would have seemed natural to the composition and reading of an oral poem—alliteration, formulaic repetition, first-person discourse—could become strange when that poem became an inscribed object, viewed from a distance.

Stanley Greenfield and Adrien Bonjour have shown that formulaic themes, such as that of "exile" or the "beasts of battle," did not fit into an established semantic role but had a variety of specific meanings according to their context.[58] In manuscript form, the poems they discuss—*Beowulf*, *The Wanderer*, and *The Seafarer*—are products of a literate cultural environment. Following Bäuml's analysis, the deviance of the formulae from any consistent use or meaning would be a result of the poems' inscription, and the "distancing" it brought about. The written texts could refer to the orality they contained by evoking a familiar theme and raising audience expectations, and then self-consciously manipulate that formula, placing it in quotation marks within its new environment. The use of first-person speech, as in *The Wanderer*, also opens up and reveals a distance between the poem, its speakers—author, narrators, fictional characters—and its audience. When "I" is read, a situation of direct speech is imagined, but the author, who wrote "I" in the past, is now absent and has no more reality than the depicted narrator or character. Bäuml attributes the development of the "poetic I," as well as the unexpected use of formulae, to the "fixity and independent existence" of a written text; these narrative structures though, are perhaps more the result of repetition than inscription. If a poem were repeated after the time of its first enunciation, a distance would exist between the time of its composition and that of its performance, as well as between its two speakers. The poem would already have gained an independent existence, without having been written; the two modes of transmission are not distinct, but flow into each other. The other crucial quality that Bäuml sees as arising at the time of writing is a text's "fixity," but as Katherine O'Brien O'Keeffe has shown, Old English poetry continued to change after it had been inscribed. The irony and recognition of distance that Bäuml describes are present in Old English written poetry, but they do not define a firm difference between oral and written. Instead, the irony produces another "voice" in the poem, and the "dialogic" text that results displays an awareness of its existence at a transitional stage of literacy.[59]

We can only know Old English oral poetry through the traces of its reuse left in the manuscript poems. Yet these traces are so prevalent that it is also impossible to know the written poetry without the oral. Neither can be imagined except in the context of the other, and the poems themselves speak of this interconnection. The nature of the representation of the oral poetic past in Old English written poetry raises questions of concepts of time and memory. This poetry does not draw from the past as if from something distinct from itself; rather it carries its past with it. Like a bricoleur, the poet searches through a storehouse of what has already been said when faced with the project of constructing another poem, or as Davis says of cavedrawings, "the artist threads his latest work through the tangled fabric of his earlier" (132). The structure of the poetry suggests a conception of time as a continuum. This is coherent with Gadamer's concept of history as a "continuing tradition"; at the same time that "historical consciousness" recognizes temporal distinctions, it returns to a position of reintegration.[60] Past affects present and present past, just as the most recent inscription on the cave wall does not leave untouched, but alters, what has been drawn before.

Afterword: Tracing Signs of Elusion

I conceive of my "tracing" of a hermeneutics as both the suggestive, tentative drawing of an outline and the tracking of signs—perceptible marks indicating methods of signification. The two activities—following a path and making one—coincide in the meanings of both the Modern English verb "to trace" and the Old English "spyrigean." One aspect of an Anglo-Saxon interpretive practice can be traced through a specific use of this verb in two Old English texts. Tracks are superimposed with written words when "spyrigean" creates a literary metaphor whereby a written text is likened to tracks left behind and reading is seen as deciphering those tracks. In Alfred's *Preface* to Gregory's *Pastoral Care*, the king writes of the great wisdom of previous scholars which is incomprehensible to later generations:

> Her mon mæg giet gesion hiora swæð, ac we him ne cunnon
> æfterspyrigean, forðæm we habbað nu ægðer forlæten ge þone welan ge
> þone wisdom, forðæmþe we noldon to ðæm spore mid ure mode onlutan.[1]

Latin books are the footprints of their elders that present scholars are not able to follow because they did not want to learn that other language (to bend their minds to that track). Writing is imaged as a sign of a former presence and of an irreparable absence. Reading fails—"we ne him cunnon æfter spyrigean"—because reader and text lack a common linguistic framework; in Alfred's description there is no Gadamerian merging of horizons.

"Spyrigean" describes the more successful creation of a verbal track in the "Bible" riddle (riddle No. 26). The speaking object tells of its production:

> ond mec fugles wyn
> geond speddropum   spyrede geneahhe,
> ofer brunne brerd,   beamtelge swealg,
> streames dæle,   stop eft on mec,
> siþade sweartlast.   (7b–11a)[2]

The absence of the writer is glossed over—not lamented as it was in Alfred's *Preface*—since the act of writing is attributed to his or her instrument ("fugles wyn" ["the joy of the bird," "a quill"]), and its product is a text that can be read. The presence of the book is emphasized through its voice that directly addresses the reader, and the readable text bridges the gap between her or him and the writer. In the riddle as in Alfred's *Preface*, though, the metaphor associating written words with a track foregrounds the mediatory nature of writing. Its materiality—the physical marks which construct it—is stressed; its opacity must be worked through and may, as in the *Preface*, present an impenetrable barrier. Reading involves deciphering the trace of a former presence.

I have attempted to decipher methods of reading and to trace strategies for interpretation rather than drawing bold outlines that would conclusively define interpretive categories. This refusal of absolute definition in describing an Anglo-Saxon hermeneutics is consistent with an elusion of definitive statement within the poetry and pictorial art. My three chapters considering the places of the reader, the frame, and the past in Anglo-Saxon texts have all articulated a fluidity of signification, a lack of clear distinction. The reader of *The Wanderer*, faced by multifaceted identity and scattered scenes, has no fixed location. The peripheral, digressive stories within *Beowulf* are at once framed by the poem and located on the border between audience and text. Past flows into present when inscribed Old English poetry reveals its process of composition and reinvokes the subjectivity of composer and reader, a characteristic usually attributed to oral storytelling. This fluidity of signification complicates the reading process, and has created many of the unanswerable questions facing present-day Old English literary criticism.

Recent critical theory has provided a framework within which to rethink the significance of these questions. The postmodern, writes Linda Hutcheon, is a "problematizing force in our culture today: it raises questions about (or renders problematic) the commonsensical and the 'natural.'"[3] Old English poetry, encountered by a present-day reader educated to appreciate literature's originality, continuity of plot, and coherence of character, does not seem at all "natural." Its gaps have had to be filled in and its problems glossed over in order to make it fit the pattern prescribed by modern reading practices. Anglo-Saxon texts do not need to be problematized; the problems are already there asking to be acknowledged and explored. The methods by which postmodern theory deconstructs the apparently "common-sensical" and "natural" offer an alternative way to read Old English poems. Although late twentieth-century theory may seem an odd framework for late tenth-century texts, it is no more so than the "expressive-realist"[4] mold that, through convention, has come to seem natural. Late twentieth-century theory has the virtues of being unrestrictive and particularly responsive to the problems of Old English texts; moreover, postmodern theory has shaped my own preconceptions, and it would be inconsistent with its purpose for a hermeneutic study to deny its own interests.

This critical theory has as one of its concerns the rethinking of conventional conceptual categories. In focusing on the problems presented by Old English poetry, I have continually found myself describing the blurring of boundaries: between self and other, the central and the peripheral, past and present, oral and written. These difficulties occur at places of mediation in the poetry, where reading is shaped. They represent the recurring questions addressed by scholars of Old English literature: how many speakers are there in *The Wanderer*, how do we account for the frequent and lengthy digressions in *Beowulf*, is the poetry the product of oral-formulaic composition? To this list could be added the merging of Christian and pagan ideologies in *Beowulf* and other poems. The verse consistently rejects interpretive attempts to organize its concepts and structures into pairs of opposites. Perhaps if an Anglo-Saxon aesthetic were to be described, it would be one of plurality and enigma.

In harmony with what I perceive as a blurring of boundaries in Anglo-Saxon texts, my interpretations have deliberately transgressed boundaries between kinds of representation: conceptual barriers between "genres" of poetry and between poetic and pictorial texts. Fundamental to my study of signification has been another, similar transgression. I have insisted on the semantic interaction of representation and design, two aspects of Old English poetry that have traditionally been examined separately.[5] Verbal and visual Anglo-Saxon texts share a predominance of ornamentation, an elaboration of structure, which indicates that their form is not subordinate to and separable from their meaning. Ornament semantically overlaps with and touches narrative or figural representation in the same way that the interlace, geometric pattern, or acanthus design of a manuscript border visually extends into the image it adorns. The blurring of compositional, structural, and conceptual borders suggested by Old English poetry can be answered by a reading practice that rejects absolute distinctions and refuses the impulse to categorize.

The concept of culturally shaped perception, and the way this perception might simultaneously affect structures of composition and of reading, has been my point of return. A reader brings expectations to a text, and I suspect that those of an Anglo-Saxon audience were very different from our own. The briefest encounter with Old English poetry entices us to discover a different way of reading. In looking at the compositional structures it shares with the contemporary pictorial art, I have suggested a way of reading the poetry that reflects specific cultural settings. Relationships articulated by kinship and community, and situations of reading—both its physical location within the gathering of a community and its oral or written transmission—affect the compositional form of the poetry, and also, I suggest, modes of textual understanding. Concepts of identity, narrative limitation, and chronology, as represented in Old English poetry, do not accord with modern expectations; difficulties in interpreting the texts reflect these differences. My book is an attempt to participate in a reconceptualization of Old English poetry, within the context of recent critical theories that provoke readings less regimented, more responsive to difference.

Notes

Introduction

1. Jonathan Culler offers an informative critique of recent theories of reading and places them within a context of interpretation's historical interest in the effects of texts on readers; see *On Deconstruction: Theory and Criticism after Structuralism* (Ithaca, N.Y., 1982), pp. 31–43.

2. "The Death of an Author," in *Image, Music, Text*, trans. Stephen Heath (New York, 1977), p. 146; original publication: "La mort d'auteur," *Manteia* 5 (1968), 12–17.

3. Allen Frantzen (*Desire for Origins: New Language, Old English, and Teaching the Tradition* [New Brunswick, N.J., and London, 1990], esp. pp. 83–94) is one of several scholars to have recently lamented the slowness of Anglo-Saxon studies in recognizing the importance of postmodern critical theory to its discipline. I discuss his critique of the present state of this scholarship, as well as those of Gillian Overing and Seth Lerer, below, (pp. 13–15).

In the Preface to his *Allegories of War: Language and Violence in Old English Poetry* (Ann Arbor, Mich., 1989), John P. Hermann describes the state of the discipline at the time of his writing as being determined by "the powerful and entrenched philological tradition that has nurtured—and stunted—Old English studies over the last two decades" (p. v). His deconstruction of Old English Christian poetry's categories of opposition challenges this tradition, engaging instead in an alternative interpretive practice responsive to the texts' "rhetorical specificity" (200).

Stephen Nichols provides a concise, critical overview of the interests and biases of medieval textual scholarship, in general, since the nineteenth century ("Introduction: Philology in a Manuscript Culture," *Speculum* 65:1 [1990], 1–10).

4. See Frantzen, esp. pp. 83–94.

5. "From Work to Text," in *Image, Music, Text*, p. 160.

6. Paul Zumthor writes that in oral poetry—I shall discuss the significance of oral vestiges in Old English written verse—there exists no "authentic" text:

"From one performance to the next, we glide from nuance to nuance or to sudden mutation; where is there, in this deteriorated state, the demarcation between what is still the 'work' and what is already no longer the 'work'?" (*Oral Poetry: An Introduction*, in Theory and History of Literature, vol. 70, trans. Kathryn Murphy-Judy [Minneapolis, 1990], p. 203.)

7. Martin Irvine writes, for example: "Old English poems present a significant difficulty for literary theory in that most of these poems presuppose a Latin-literate textual community and a system of discursive practices from Latin tradition imposed upon, or mediating, an earlier oral and Germanic textuality." ("Anglo-Saxon Literary Theory Exemplified in Old English Poems: Interpreting the Cross in *The Dream of the Rood* and *Elene*," *Style* 20:2 [Summer, 1986], 158.)

Although this list is by no means comprehensive, the following scholarship exemplifies studies undertaken in this area: Peter Clemoes, "Mens absentia cogitans in *The Seafarer* and *The Wanderer*," in D. Pearsall and R. A. Waldron, eds., *Medieval Literature and Civilization: Studies in Memory of G. N. Garmonsway* (London, 1969), pp. 62–77; James W. Earl, "Christian Tradition in the Old English *Exodus*," *Neuphilologische Mitteilungen* 71 (1970), 541–70, and "The Typological Structure of *Andreas*," in J. D. Niles, ed., *Old English Literature in Context: Ten Essays* (Cambridge, 1980), pp. 66–89; John P. Hermann, *Allegories of War*; Anne L. Klinck, *The Old English Elegies: A Critical Edition and Genre Study* (Montreal and Kingston, 1992), pp. 231–38; and Seth Lerer, *Literacy and Power in Anglo-Saxon Literature* (Lincoln, Neb., and London, 1991).

8. *Truth and Method* (New York, 1982); trans. of *Wahrheit und Methode: Grundzüge einer philosophischen Hermeneutik* (Tübingen, 1960), 272–73. All further references are to this edition.

9. "Rhetoric, Hermeneutics, and the Critique of Ideology: Metacritical Comments on *Truth and Method*," in Kurt Mueller-Vollmer, ed., *The Hermeneutics Reader* (New York, 1989), p. 284; trans. of *Theorie Diskussion: Hermeneutik und Ideologiekritik* (Frankfurt a/M, 1971).

10. *Textualities: Between Hermeneutics and Deconstruction* (New York and London, 1994), p. 22.

11. In addition to Silverman's recent volume (cited above), which specifically addresses the problem of reconciling Gadamer's and Derrida's interpetive practice, an introductory bibliography on this topic would include: Ernst Behler, "Deconstruction versus Hermeneutics: Derrida and Gadamer on Text and Interpretation," *Southern Humanities Review* 21:3 (1987), 201–23; and Diane P. Michelfelder and Richard E. Palmer, eds., *Dialogue and Deconstruction: The Gadamer-Derrida Encounter* (Albany, 1989).

12. Jacques Derrida, "Parergon," in *The Truth in Painting*, trans. Geoff Bennington and Ian McLeod (Chicago and London, 1987), pp. 77–78.: "[I]t will be said that not all frames are, or have been, or will be square, rectangular, or quadrangu-

lar figures, nor even simply angular. Tables and tableaux (Tafel) likewise not. This is true: a critical and systematic and typological history of framing seems possible and necessary. But the angle in general, the quadrangular in particular will not be just one of its objects among others. Everything that is written here is valid for the logic of parergonal bordering *in general*, but the privilege of 'cadre' [frame], though it seems more fortunate in the Latin than in the Germanic languages, is not fortuitous. . . ." All further references will be to this edition.

13. Gadamer has elsewhere expressed less certainty (see Behler, p. 208). Perhaps his confidence reflects the *potential* comprehensibility of the sign, although, in fact, understanding may never be achieved because of the inevitable "polysemy" of the hermeneutic act. The reader's understanding will always change in time; comprehension is a process. As Gadamer writes, "the conversation that we are is one that never ends. No word is the last word, just as there is no first word" ("Letter to Dallmayr," trans. Richard Palmer and Diane Michelfelder, in their *Dialogue and Deconstruction*, p. 95). This discrepancy represents, at least apparently, a contradiction in Gadamer's thought; see Fred R. Dallmayr, "Prelude: Hermeneutics and Deconstruction: Gadamer and Derrida in Dialogue," in *Dialogue and Deconstruction*, pp. 84–85.

14. "Rhetoric, Hermeneutics, and the Critique of Ideology," p. 285.

15. "Structure, Sign, and Play in the Human Sciences," in his *Writing and Difference*, trans. Alan Bass (Chicago, 1978), p. 292.

16. "Prelude," p. 83.

17. Adeline C. Bartlett, *The Larger Rhetorical Patterns in Anglo-Saxon Poetry* (New York, 1935); John Leyerle, "The Interlace Structure of *Beowulf*," *University of Toronto Quarterly* 37 (1967), 1–17.

18. Catherine Belsey, *Critical Practice* (London, 1980), p. 17.

19. "The Storyteller: Reflections on the Works of Nikolai Leskov," in *Illuminations: Essays and Reflections*, ed. Hannah Arendt, trans. Harry Zohn (New York, 1969), p. 92.

20. (Carbondale and Edwardsville, Ill., 1990).

21. (New Brunswick, N.J., and London, 1990).

22. (Albany, 1991).

23. (Lincoln, Neb., and London, 1991).

24. Carol Braun Pasternack's *The Textuality of Old English Poetry* (Cambridge and New York, 1995) has been published since the completion of *Representation and Design*. I am familiar with Pasternack's previously published articles and am certain this recent work offers an exciting rethinking of textual structures and their cultural environments.

Chapter 1

1. Traditionally, these poems have been given the label *elegies*, a term Stanley Greenfield defines as "a relatively short reflective or dramatic poem embodying a contrasting pattern of loss and consolation, ostensibly based upon a specific personal experience or observation, and expressing an attitude towards that experience" ("The Old English Elegies," in E. G. Stanley, ed., *Continuations and Beginnings: Studies in Old English Literature* [London, 1966], p. 143). There are several problems, however, with this categorization. As early as 1942, B. J. Timmer ("The Elegiac Mood in Old English Poetry," *English Studies* 24 [1942], 33–44) questioned whether the poems (those I have mentioned, as well as *The Ruin, The Rhyming Poem*, and *The Exile's Prayer* [*Resignation* in *Anglo-Saxon Poetic Records*]) could be included under the *Encylopaedia Britannica*'s definition of an elegy—"a short poem of lamentation or regret, called forth by the decease of a beloved or revered person, or by a general sense of the pathos of mortality." (p. 33) After examining each of the "elegies" he concludes, "If, however, we had better avoid the name of elegies for the poems discussed above, we are certainly justified in speaking of an elegiac mood in Old English poetry, but then we should not confine ourselves to the nine poems mentioned here. The whole of *Beowulf*, for instance, is pervaded by an elegiac spirit and it is also expressed in many other places in old English epic poetry" (41). For a definition to be meaningful it should distinguish characteristics common to the category being defined and limited to that category. Although Timmer has argued that the term *elegy* fulfils neither of these functions, critics continue to group these poems under that heading. T. A. Shippey, despite his criticism of the term as "vague enough to be inoffensive if unhelpful" (53), binds the poems together in a chapter entitled "Wisdom and Experience: The Old English 'Elegies'" (*Old English Verse* [London, 1972], pp. 53–79).

Besides the specific problems with the coherence as a group of Old English poems called "elegies," theoretical questions have been raised lately as to the validity of "genre criticism" in general. Literary criticism has gone through a radical change of focus that has involved (as one of its aspects) studying the text from the point of view of the reader, rather than the author. This reorientation draws into question the function of genre divisions. Jonathan Culler describes a genre as "a set of expectations, a set of instructions about the type of coherence one is to look for and the ways in which sequences are to be read" ("Towards a Theory of Non-Genre Literature," in Raymond Federman, ed., *Surfiction: Fiction Now . . . and Tomorrow* [Chicago, 1975], p. 255). He explains the difference between the traditional (empirical) view of genres and the view he is offering in its place: "There is . . . an alternative view of genres: that they are simply taxonomic categories in which we place works that share certain features. Since every work has properties, every work, perforce, could be placed in some genre. . . . This view of genres seems singularly unhelpful. To treat them as taxonomic classes is to obscure their function as norms in the process of reading" (256). If *The Wanderer, The Wife's Lament*, and *Deor* are read with the preconception that they are "passionate" poems, the "products of individual experience" (Shippey, p. 53), these common features will be stressed and any deviant aspects explained away. But the difficulty of reading these poems has significance and should not be masked; they display what Culler calls "the essence of literature"—"not representation, not a communicative transparency, but an opacity, a resistance to recuperation which exercises sensibility and intelligence" (258).

See Anne L. Klinck, *The Old English Elegies: A Critical Edition and Genre Study* (Montreal and Kingston, 1992), pp. 11–12 and 223–51, for a discussion of the history of *elegy* and the significance of the term as a description of this group of Old English poems. Klinck is of the opinion that "the notion of genre . . . is always an important concept" (p. 224), and that the categorization of these nine poems as elegies is "useful" and "convenient" as a way of understanding certain common themes (p. 11). She concludes by offering her own definition of the term: "Old English elegy is a discourse arising from a powerful sense of absence, of separation from what is desired, expressed through characteristic words and themes, and shaping itself by echo and leitmotiv into a poem that moves from disquiet to some kind of acceptance" (246).

2. *The Wanderer* survives only in the Exeter Book, a West-Saxon manuscript written in the second half of the tenth century. Patrick W. Conner considers various arguments for the dating of the manuscript and argues, on the basis of a close, comparative study of its letter-forms, for a date between 950 and 968 (*Anglo-Saxon Exeter: A Tenth-Century Cultural History*, Studies in Anglo-Saxon History IV [Woodbridge, Suffolk, 1993], pp. 54–94). The Junius Manuscript was probably written and illustrated at Canterbury in the early eleventh century (David Wilson, *Anglo-Saxon Art*, pp. 180–81).

3. In *Between Languages: The Uncooperative Text in Early Welsh and Old English Nature Poetry*, Sarah Lynn Higley also adopts the principle of reading early medieval poetry with an acceptance of the texts' difficulties and with a consideration of interpretive perspectives. Since she herself "read[s] Old English through the lens of the Welsh" (128)—and finds the latter more disjunctive, abstract, and ambiguous—Higley's conclusions are quite different from my own: "[T]he Old English elegies, long thought to be disjointed and cryptic, are actually invested in explanation and disclosure to a degree that the comparable Welsh poems are not" (University Park, Pa., 1993, p. 4).

4. Renaissance perspective—a complex, ideologically defined concept—deserves a much more thorough and sensitive treatment than I can give it here. At the same time, I do not intend to reduce it to a straw man against which to argue. I (in face of Derrida's precautions about the danger of diversion through the example) follow theorists such as Roland Barthes, Norman Bryson, and Stephen Heath in taking Renaissance perspective as an example of a visual code having implications for interpretive processes.

5. Norman Bryson, *Vision and Painting: The Logic of the Gaze* (London, 1983), p. 104.

6. Roland Barthes, "Diderot, Brecht, Eisenstein," in *Image, Music, Text*, trans. Stephen Heath (New York, 1977), p. 69.

7. Christian Metz, "The Imaginary Signifier," trans. Ben Brewster, *Screen* 16:20 (1975), 14–76; rpt. in his *The Imaginary Signifier: Psychoanalysis and the Cinema*, trans. Celia Britton, et al. (Bloomington, Ind., 1982), pp. 1–98; Stephen Heath, "Lessons from Brecht," *Screen* 15:2 (1974), 103–28, and *Questions of Cinema* (Bloomington, Ind., 1981).

8. Heath, "Lessons from Brecht," pp. 117–18.

9. Conventions governing Renaissance and post-Renaissance perspective in painting are not applicable, from the outset, to eleventh-century manuscript art; the image of a viewer standing before a painting cannot be translated to describe a reader's position relative to a manuscript page.

10. Rosemary Chaplan discusses sightlines in the Junius drawings in her unpublished essay, "A Comparison between the Junius 11 Adam and Eve Sequence and the Same Sequence in the San Marco Mosaics and Several Touronian Bibles" (1985).

11. In contrast to a text whose chronology must be resolved by the reader is the system of "classical narrative cinema" as described by Stephen Heath: "The coherence of any text depends on a sustained equilibrium of new informations, points of advance, and anaphoric recalls, ties that make fast, hold together. One part of the particular economy is the exploitation of narrative in film in the interests of an extreme tendency towards coalescence, a tightness of totalization" (*Questions of Cinema*, pp. 123–24).

12. G. P. Krapp and E. Van K. Dobbie, eds., *The Exeter Book, Anglo-Saxon Poetic Records*, vol. 3 (New York, 1936). All quotations are from this edition. Hereafter, all references to this series of editions will be cited as ASPR. "So spoke the wanderer, mindful of hardships, cruel slaughters, the deaths of dear kinsmen" (6–7). "So spoke the one wise in mind, he sat apart at counsel" (111). All translations are my own.

13. "The Wanderer: Theme and Structure," *Journal of English and Germanic Philology* 42 (1943), 516–38.

14. "*The Wanderer*: A Reconsideration of Theme and Structure," *Journal of English and Germanic Philology* 50 (1951), 464. See also his "The Old English Elegies," esp. pp. 146–53, and "Min, Sylf, and 'Dramatic Voices in *The Wanderer* and *The Seafarer*,'" *Journal of English and Germanic Philology* 68 (1969), 212–20.

15. "Dramatic Voices in *The Wanderer* and *The Seafarer*," in J. B. Bessinger, Jr., and R. P. Creed, eds., *Franciplegius: Medieval and Linguistic Studies in Honor of Francis Peabody Magoun, Jr.* (New York, 1965), pp. 164–93; rpt. in J. B. Bessinger, Jr., and S. J. Kahrl, eds., *Essential Articles for the Study of Old English Poetry* (Hamden, Conn., 1968), pp. 533–70; and "Second Thoughts on the Interpretation of *The Seafarer*," *Anglo-Saxon England* 3 (1974), 75–86, esp. 75–76.

16. *The Wanderer* (London, 1969), pp. 79–80.

17. "On the Identity of the Wanderer," in Martin Green, ed., *The Old English Elegies: New Essays in Criticism and Research* (London and Toronto, 1983), pp. 82–95.

18. "*The Wanderer, The Seafarer*, and the Genre of Planctus," in Lewis E. Nicholson and Dolores Warwick Frese, eds., *Anglo-Saxon Poetry: Essays in Appreciation* (Notre Dame, Ind., 1975), pp. 192–207. See note 1, above, regarding the problematic implications of genre criticism. Anne L. Klinck documents theories regarding speech boundaries in *The Wanderer* in her *The Old English Elegies: A Critical Edition and Genre Study*, pp. 107, 118, 123–24, and 126. See also Lois Bragg, *The Lyric Speakers of Old English Poetry* (Rutherford, Madison, Teaneck, N.J., 1992), pp. 128–35.

19. Carol Braun Pasternack's description of the text's way of indicating "speaking positions or perspectives framed and juxtaposed" (117–20) parallels, to an extent, my interpretation of the poem's types of speech as productive of a shifting perspective ("Anonymous Polyphony and *The Wanderer*'s Textuality," *Anglo-Saxon England* 20 [1991], 99–122).

20. I include lines 1–5 (about a solitary man ["anhaga"]), 12–18 (about a nobleman ["eorl"]), 30–57 (one who has few beloved protectors ["lyt hafað / leofra geholena"]), 62–74 and 88–91 (a wise man ["wita" 65b, "frod in ferðe," 90a]), and 112–15 (one who keeps his pledge ["his treowe gehealdeþ"]).

21. The most obvious exception occurs in lines 12–18, introduced by "Ic to soþe wat / þæt . . ." ("I know truly that . . ."). I will discuss this passage later as an example of the merging of voices.

22. "Often, at each dawn, I had to lament my sadness alone. Now there is no one alive to whom I dare openly speak my heart."

23. "[S]o I, often wretched, deprived of my homeland, far from noble kin, have had to seal my heart with fetters, since long ago I covered my generous lord in the darkness of earth, and, wretched, journeyed from there, winter-sad, over the binding of the waves; sad for a hall, I sought a giver of treasure, sought far and near where I might find in a meadhall one who would know my thought, or would comfort me, friendless, allure with delights."

24. "Therefore, I cannot think for all this world why my heart does not grow dark when I contemplate the life of noblemen, how they suddenly left the floor, the brave young retainers."

25. Ricoeur describes the significance of pronouns, tenses, adverbs of time and place, and demonstratives: "The inner structure of the sentence refers back to its speaker through grammatical procedures, which linguists call 'shifters.'" (*Interpretation Theory. Discourse and the Surplus of Meaning* [Fort Worth, Texas 1976], p. 13.) Norman Bryson describes these same parts of speech according to their role in classical rhetoric: "Deictic (from 'deiknonei,' to show)" refers to "utterances that

contain information concerning the locus of utterance. . . . Deixis is utterance in carnal form and points back directly (deiknonei) to the body of the speaker" (*Vision and Painting*, pp. 88–89).

Suzanne Fleischman speaks of the importance of "the 'little words' of vernacular grammar" to New Philological research and suggests that "it would be of interest to investigate a possible correlation between the passage from oral to written transmission of the cultural legacy and the use of temporal versus spatial adverbs as articulators of discourse" ("The Discourse of the Medieval Text," *Speculum* 65:1 [1990], 33). For a discussion of deixis in several Old English poems, see Sarah Lynn Higley, "The Vanishing Point: Deixis and Conjunction" (*Between Languages*, pp. 119–48).

26. In the section describing the thoughts of "one who has few beloved protectors" (30–57), "ðonne" and "hwilum ær in geardagum" describe time, and "þær" describes place.

27. "I know truly that it is a fitting custom in a nobleman that he bind fast his heart, hold in his thoughts, whatever he may think. One who is weary of heart may not withstand fate, nor the troubled mind provide help. Therefore, those eager for glory often bind fast the sadness in their breast."

28. "Often the solitary one awaits mercy, the kindness of the lord, although he, sad in spirit, for a long time had to move with his hands the frost-cold sea, throughout the waterway, had to walk the paths of an exile. Fate is very resolute!"

29. Alain Renoir uses this image to describe *The Ruin:* "*The Ruin* stands out from the other Old English elegies insofar as it is a series of tableaux rather than a narrative or philosophical monologue" ("The Old English Ruin: Contrastive Structure and Affective Impact," in Martin Green, ed., *The Old English Elegies: New Essays in Criticism and Research* [London and Toronto, 1983], p. 149). I find the description appropriate to *The Wanderer* because the poem represents neither a continuous narrative nor a psychologically unified narrator. Its scenes are disconnected.

30. "It seems to him in his mind that he embraces and kisses his lord, and lays his hands and head on his knee, as he once, in days gone by, benefited from the throne."

31. "[D]ark waves, seabirds bathing, spreading their feathers, frost and snow falling, mixed with hail."

32. "[H]e greets joyfully, looks upon eagerly the companions of men. They swim away again! The spirit of the floating ones does not bring many familiar songs."

33. "[T]hroughout this earth walls stand, blown upon by wind, covered in frost, the ruined buildings. The winehalls crumble, rulers lie deprived of joy, all the troop fallen, the proud by the wall."

34. "Now the wall, wonderfully high, decorated with serpentine patterns, stands as a trace of the beloved troop of retainers. A multitude of spears took away the noblemen, weapons greedy for slaughter, fate the renowned, and storms batter the cliffs, a falling snowstorm binds the earth, the tumult of winter, when darkness comes, the shadow of night grows dark, sends from the north a fierce hailstorm, in malice to the warriors."

35. See Peter Clemoes, "Action in *Beowulf* and our Perception of it," in Daniel G. Calder, ed., *Old English Poetry: Essays on Style* (Berkeley, 1979), pp. 147–68. "Old English poetic narrative does not have what I would call 'audience perspective'; in other words, description is not directed toward the viewpoint, outside the scene, which we as hearers or readers of a poem might be supposed to have" (147).

36. The wise man's description of a world in ruins is presented as direct speech, but as discussed above, he does not refer to himself in the first person. He is not a character like the "eardstapa," but the personification of a type.

37. See, among many others, Lorraine Lancaster's two-part article "Kinship in Anglo-Saxon Society," *British Journal of Sociology* 9 (1958), 230–49 and 359–77, and H. R. Loyn, "Kinship in Anglo-Saxon England," *Anglo-Saxon England* 3 (1974), 197–209.

38. "Landless men who had been serving in another shire were to be harboured by a kinsman on the condition that the latter should be responsible for their misdeeds," Lancaster (369), with reference to II Aethelstan 8. In legal disputes kinsmen could also stand surety for an individual, or attest to her or his innocence (Lancaster, 370; laws of Athelstan).

39. See note 23 above for translation.

40. In Lacan's "mirror phase," the infant seeks a unified sense of self through identification with a reflection that is perceived as being at once the same as and better than the infant's actual state. The perceived unity surpasses the subject's real state of helplessness and fragmentation, making the imaginary more attractive than the real. "The *mirror stage* is a drama whose internal thrust is precipitated from insufficiency to anticipation—and which manufactures for the subject, caught up in the lure of spatial identification, the succession of phantasies that extends from a fragmented body-image to a form of its totality that I shall call orthopaedic—and, lastly, to the assumption of the armour of an alienating identity, which will mark with its rigid structure the subject's entire mental development" (Jacques Lacan, "The Mirror-phase as Formative of the Function of the I as revealed in Psychoanalytic Experience," trans. Alan Sheridan in *Ecrits: A Selection* [London, 1977], p. 4).

41. "The Voice in the Cinema: The Articulation of Body and Space," *Yale French Studies* 60 (1980), 33–50. Doane examines the ways in which the whole cinematic apparatus is structured to mask that medium's heterogeneity. I am focusing on the apparent unity of the fictional character because of the particular problems of reading *The Wanderer*.

42. "To disturb the achieved relations of sound and image in the [cinematic] apparatus is to disturb the performance, to break the whole coherence of vision" (Heath, *Questions of Cinema*, p. 121).

43. Christian Metz describes the screen as the "other mirror . . . a veritable psychical substitute" for the Lacanian mirror ("The Imaginary Signifier," p. 15); he elaborates, "the cinema only gives [the audiovisual] in effigy inaccessible from the outset, in a primordial elsewhere, infinitely desirable (= never possessible), on another scene which is that of absence and which nonetheless represents the absent in detail, thus making it very present but by a different itinerary" (62).

44. See Lois Bragg, *The Lyric Speakers of Old English Poetry*, for a very thoughtful, deliberately subjective consideration of the differences between the reading situations of Anglo-Saxon and twentieth-century audiences of Old English lyric poetry.

45. Suzanne Fleischman observes that "[t]he oral mental habits of all languages that have not grammaticalized writing necessarily leave their mark on linguistic structure" ("Philology, Linguistics, and the Discourse of the Medieval Text," *Speculum* 65:1 [1990], 22). John Miles Foley has written extensively on what I refer to as "vestiges of the oral in the written"; see, for example, *The Singer of Tales in Performance* (Bloomington, Ind., 1995), esp. chapter 3, "The Rhetorical Persistence of Traditional Forms," pp. 60–98.

46. Alain Renoir comments on this question: "I personally like to think that some of the poems in the *Exeter Book* are the product of oral performance, but I should be at a loss to demonstrate that anyone ever heard an oral performance of these poems in the form in which they have been recorded there or, indeed, in any form at all. . . . [Yet] unless we suppose Leofric to have wanted his clergy and visiting scholars to read Christian and edifying poetry composed in a rhetorical tradition alien and therefore meaningless to them, we must assume the oral-formulaic tradition of that poetry to have been familiar enough to the intended *readers* to warrant the donation." (*A Key to Old Poems*, pp. 78–79)
    Patrick Wormald considers the "restricted" spread of literacy in "The Uses of Literacy in Anglo-Saxon England and Its Neighbours," *Transactions of the Royal Historical Society*, 5th series, 27 (1977), 95–114. See also Susan Kelly, "Anglo-Saxon Lay Society and the Written Word," in Rosamond McKitterick, ed., *The Uses of Literacy in Early Medieval Europe* (Cambridge, 1990), pp. 36–62. For a study of representations of literacy in Anglo-Saxon literature, see Seth Lerer, *Literacy and Power in Anglo-Saxon Literature*, esp. chapter 2 ("The Beautiful Letters: Authority and Authorship in Asser and King Alfred," pp. 61–96); Lerer reconsiders the implications of Alfred's *Preface* to Gregory's *Pastoral Care*, a text often treated as the central document in understanding Anglo-Saxon literacy.

47. When discussing the Junius drawings I said that it would be anachronistic to speak of them as deviating from codes of Renaissance perspective; the same principle is at work here. These Anglo-Saxon texts do not intentionally subvert, but simply predate, our conventional reading structures. To describe the different con-

texts of the two, I shall say that the postmodern text faces a once "whole," now fragmented, subject—a reader in parts, while the Old English poem faces a group—a reader as part of a community.

Pasternack ("Anonymous Polyphony and *The Wanderer*'s Textuality") also reads *The Wanderer* in light of twentieth-century texts: "[O]rganic structure is not universal—it is a quality cultivated for a time in printed literature—and *The Wanderer*'s polyphony, far from being unique, is conventional for its time. Fortunately, this kind of text has come around again in modernism, and modernist theory clarifies its operation" (103). She defines "modernist" as referring to literature and criticism that has "challenged ideas of coherence and unity" (103, n. 17).

48. Some elements of Brian Stock's concept of a "textual community"—the function of memory, the achievement of agreement, the creation of a bond—are relevant to the oral reading situation I describe; see *The Implications of Literacy: Written Language and Models of Interpretation in the Eleventh and Twelfth Centuries* (Princeton, N.J., 1983) and "Medieval Literacy, Linguistic Theory, and Social Organization," *New Literary History* 16:1 (1984), 13–29.

John Miles Foley describes the Anglo-Saxon "interpretive community" that was created through the oral-traditional history of the poetry. The audience would have been "unified by the act of (re-)making and (re-)'reading' traditional verbal art" ("Texts That Speak to Readers Who Hear: Old English Poetry and the Languages of Oral Tradition," in Allen Frantzen, ed., *Speaking Two Languages*, p. 150).

Stanley Greenfield speculates that formulaic expressions of exile would unite the experiences of exiled characters ("The Formulaic Expression of the Theme of 'Exile' in Anglo-Saxon Poetry," in J. B. Bessinger, Jr., and S. J. Kahrl, eds., *Essential Articles for the Study of Old English Poetry* [Hamden, Conn., 1968], p. 359). Through this process, as well, the individual sufferer is understood as part of an experiential community.

49. In *The Audience of Beowulf* (Oxford, 1951), a study whose overall concern is a reconsideration of the date of the poem, Dorothy Whitelock reconstructs an audience ("the people whom [the poet] had in mind," [3]) already educated to understand the poet's Christian allusions and even his specifically poetic expressions of Christian concepts. Their frame of reference would also have included a knowledge of Scandanavian history and legend: "A well-informed audience would call to mind the whole tale at each reference to it" (34).

50. Within the context of a reflection upon "the art of storytelling," "the exchanging of experiences," Walter Benjamin says, "The more self-forgetful the listener is, the more deeply is what he listens to impressed upon his memory. When the rhythm of the work has seized him, he listens to the tales in such a way that the gift of retelling them comes to him all by itself." ("The Storyteller: Reflections on the Works of Nikolai Leskov," in *Illuminations: Essays and Reflections*, ed. Hannah Arendt, trans. Harry Zohn [New York, 1969], p. 91.)

51. The gathering together of a community through the process of poetic performance is discussed by Paul Zumthor: "For this reason [the political nature of

any such performance] the oral poetic text pushes the listener to identify with the purveyor of the words that they experience in common. . . . [P]erformance unifies and unites." (*Oral Poetry*, p. 188.)

52. Pasternack reads the significance of performance differently than I. For me, it adds another layer of contradiction, while in her interpretation the speaker of the poem (a person whom she calls the "poet") supplies a unifying presence: "For the oral composition the poet is present, speaking the text, and so he or she does not need to embody a fictional speaker within the text. Rather than using such a speaker as a point of view from which to take in the text, the audience can use as their viewpoint the context of the performance and their own presence at it" ("Anonymous polyphony and *The Wanderer*'s textuality," pp. 116–17).

53. Interpreters of *The Wanderer* have considered the problem of reconciling the wanderer's praise of silence with his subsequent lament. Gerald Richman ("Speaker and Speech Boundaries in The Wanderer," *Journal of English and Germanic Philology* 81 [1982], 469–79) proposes as a solution that the verse "Swa cwæð snottor on mode" (111a) be read "so spoke the wise man in his heart," rather than "so spoke the man wise in heart". This would indicate that "the wanderer's reflections are inward" (470). This may be a solution for the silent reader, but such an interpretation would not lessen the impact of hearing a performer say "I must not speak."

54. Paul Zumthor writes: "Once the risk is accepted the spectator [of a performed poem], like the reader confronting a book, becomes implicated in an interpretation wherein nothing ensures its correctness. But, more than the reader's, the spectator's place is unstable: narrataire? narrator? these functions tend to exchange themselves endlessly at the very core of oral customs" (*Oral Poetry*, p. 183). The disorientation of the reader of *The Wanderer* can thus be understood as, in part, a reflection of the poem's history in oral performance.

55. Catherine Belsey, following Benveniste's definition of three kinds of discourse (declarative, interrogative, and imperative; Emile Benveniste, *Problems in General Linguistics* [Coral Gables, 1971]) describes an interrogative text as one which "brings points of view into unresolved collision or contradiction." Challenged by such a text, "the reader is distanced, at least from time to time, rather than wholly interpolated into a fictional world" (*Critical Practice* [London, 1980], p. 92).

56. G. P. Krapp and E. Van K. Dobbie, eds., *The Exeter Book*, ASPR, vol. 3 (New York, 1936). All numeration and quotations are from this edition. I have also referred to Craig Williamson, ed., *The Old English Riddles of the Exeter Book* (Chapel Hill, N.C., 1977). For my present purposes, I am not discussing various possible solutions to the riddles but instead accepting those most commonly held.

57. The manuscript reads "wæpen wiga"; like most editors Krapp and Dobbie have emended to the compound, which can be translated as "armed warrior." Williamson follows Moritz Trautman and A.E.H. Swaen ("The Anglo-Saxon Horn Riddles,"

Neophilologus 26 [1941], 298–302) in reading "wæpen wigan" ("the weapon of a warrior") "since [the creature-horn] carries no weapon but is the weapon itself" (*The Old English Riddles of the Exeter Book*, p. 171).

58. Marie Nelson says that in the "Horn" riddle, as well as in "Sun" (riddle No. 6) and "Storm" (riddles 1 to 3), "a riddler describes a single subject, and in spite of shifts in spatial perspective he keeps his focus on that single subject, and the repetition of the time related word 'hwilum' helps to provide a sense of continuity" ("The Rhetoric of the Exeter Book Riddles," *Speculum* 49 [July 1974]), 432–33). It seems to me rather that there is no single subject to focus on, and that "hwilum" marks points of transition without providing any temporal continuity.

59. Peter Orton compares these riddle objects to the cross in *The Dream of the Rood* in terms of "an object's misinterpretation (in human terms) of actions towards and around it" ("The Technique of Object-Personification in *The Dream of the Rood* and a Comparison with the Old English Riddles, *Leeds Studies in English* 11 [1980], p. 11).

60. Joseph Bosworth and T. Northcote Toller, *An Anglo-Saxon Dictionary* (Oxford, 1882; *Supplement* Toller, Oxford, 1921; with *Revised and Enlarged Addenda* by Alistair Campbell, Oxford, 1972).

61. Belsey, p. 59.

62. That the speaker is female is indicated by the feminine forms of the transliterated runes—"higoræ" (7–9)—and of the adjective "glado" (7).

63. "I am a marvellous creature, I change my voice: sometimes I bark like a dog, sometimes bleat like a goat, sometimes cry like a goose, sometimes yell like a hawk."

64. Several of the riddles contain visual clues; these are often runes, but in "Bow" a reverse spelling of the object's name in Latin letters introduces the poem. "Reed Pen" (No. 60) does not explicitly depend on a form of inscription for its solution, but the speaking object does identify itself through its ability to write. (See chapter 3 for a discussion of the coincidence of oral and written representation in tenth-century poetry.)

65. Quoted in Belsey, *Critical Practice*, p. 64.

66. Even without such an overt statement of the enigma the reader is surprised at the source of the speech. Marie Nelson ("The Paradox of Silent Speech in the Exeter Book Riddles," *Neophilologus* 62 [1978], 609–15) describes three riddles (No. 85, "Fish and River"; No. 48, "Chalice"; and No. 60, "Reed Pen") in which the speaker describes itself as silent: "[E]ven as [the speakers] tell us all about themselves—what their homes are like, how they live their lives, where and how they grew up—they deny that they can do what they are doing" (614).

67. Although Williamson does not explain whom he believes the "riddler" to be—the author of the poem, a persona represented in the poem, or a performer

reading it—he offers a lucid and concise description of the enigma: "In terms of the game, the riddler pretends to be the creature in question. The voice of the riddle is the voice of the unknown creature cloaked in the disguise of man. The disguise is double. The riddler (man) pretends to be the creature (not man), but the creature describes himself in typically human terms" (25).

68. She cites Chomsky's system of classifying nouns: animate or inanimate, human or nonhuman. In the latter decision, "the deciding factor . . . seems to be whether the entity designated by the noun can speak" ("The Paradox of Silent Speech . . . ," p. 609). She offers the interpretation: "[M]any of the riddles seem to suggest that their composers knew very well what the binary choices that their language gave them were, but decided that it was just too plodding to see everything on middle-earth as just one way or its opposite" (614).

69. "[T]he objects of any rational investigation have no prior existence but are thought into being. The object does not pose before the interrogating eye, for thought is not the passive perception of a general disposition, as though the object should offer to share itself, like an open fruit, both displayed and concealed by a single gesture. The act of knowing is not like listening to a discourse already constituted, a mere fiction which we have simply to translate. It is rather the elaboration of a new discourse, the articulation of a silence." (Pierre Macherey, *A Theory of Literary Production*, trans. Geoffrey Wall [London, 1978], pp. 5–6, as quoted by Belsey, p. 138.) For a summary of several other recent theories of the interplay between reader and text as subject and object see Jonathan Culler, *On Deconstruction*, pp. 69–78.

70. Williamson describes the two kinds of riddles as "the two poles of the perceptual game" (25), and says of the second, "This kind of riddle is a narrative riddle in which man retains his human identity in order to describe the miraculous identity of the riddlic creature. Still the creature that is not human is often described in human terms. . . . These narrative riddles we may call third-person riddles of description" (26).

71. See Orton, "The Technique of Object Personification in The Dream of the Rood . . . ," and Irvine, "Anglo-Saxon Literary Theory in Old English Poems" (pp. 160–64 and 171–75).

72. G. P. Krapp, eds., *The Vercelli Book*, ASPR 2 (New York, 1932). "The young hero then undressed, (that was almighty God), strong and resolute. He climbed up onto the high gallows, brave in the sight of many, when he wished to release mankind. I trembled when the warrior embraced me. But I did not dare bend to the earth. . . . "

73. In *The Wanderer*, voice and vision were similarly split as the "eardstapa" described what "other" characters saw.

74. See Peter Clemoes, "Action in *Beowulf* and Our Perception of It." Also Catherine Belsey: "The meeting between Odysseus and Nausicaa in *The Odyssey* or

the death of Priam in *The Aeneid* provide no specific position in the scene for the reader. But classic realism locates the reader in the events" (76).

75. As discussed by Orton, p. 11.

76. In the first section of the poem (before line 28), the tree is usually the object of the sentence and of the viewer's perception. At line 19, though, it begins to "bleed or sweat," at line 22 it "changes," and at line 26 it "speaks." Even in these instances when the tree is an active subject, the description of its action occurs within a *that* clause, so it is still something that the dreamer saw—an object of perception. See Carol Braun Pasternack, "Stylistic Disjunctions in 'The Dream of the Rood,'" *Anglo-Saxon England* 13 (1984), 173–75.

77. I am referring here to the cross's repeated statements during the crucifixion (lines 35–47) that it did not dare go against the Lord's word by falling upon and injuring his enemies (although the cross could have done so, and strongly desired to defend its L/ lord).

78. In "Rhetoric . . . ," Marie Nelson says: "[T]he riddles enabled or compelled members of Anglo-Saxon audiences to draw upon several areas of knowledge to find their solutions. These areas involved the heroic, patristic, and erotic perspectives of the men in the mead halls and in the monasteries, and they reflected the multiple frames of reference which were the natural result of the fusion of cultures" (421).

79. For further discussion of the significance to its interpretation of this poem's structure see: Constance B. Hieatt, "Dream Frame and Verbal Echo in *The Dream of the Rood*," *Neuphilologische Mitteilungen* 72 (1971), 251–63; Eugene R. Kintgen, "Echoic Repetition in Old English Poetry, Especially *The Dream of the Rood*," *Neuphilologische Mitteilungen* 75 (1974), 202–23; and Carol Braun Pasternack, "Stylistic disjunctions in *The Dream of the Rood*."
Pasternack's analysis is most relevant to the present discussion; she argues that the sections of the poem, demarcated by formal disjunction, each offer a particular perspective on the poem's meaning.

80. See chapter 3, for a discussion of the overlap of written and oral in tenth- and eleventh-century poetry.

81. The Brussels Cross is also inscribed, along its sides, with words resembling a passage of *The Dream of the Rood*: "Rod is min nama. Geo ic ricne cyning / bær byfigynde, bolde bestemed." (E. Van K. Dobbie, ed., *The Anglo-Saxon Minor Poems*, ASPR 6 (New York, 1942). Discussion of the Brussels Cross can be found in Bruce Dickens and Alan S. C. Ross, eds., *The Dream of the Rood*, 4th ed. (London, 1954), pp. 13–16.

82. For illustrations see plates 34–37, 121–22, and 240 in David M. Wilson, *Anglo-Saxon Art: From the Seventh Century to the Norman Conquest* (Woodstock, N.Y., 1984).

83. The Ruthwell Cross, located in a small church in Ruthwell, Dumfriesshire, stands seventeen feet, four inches tall, and is carved of sandstone. Dating the

cross has proved difficult; most recently, convincing arguments have been made assigning the construction of the sculpture to ca. 730, or less specifically, the early eighth century. See Douglas MacLean, "The Date of the Ruthwell Cross" (49–70), and Paul Meyvaert, "A New Perspective on the Ruthwell Cross: Ecclesia and Vita Monastica" (95–166), both in *The Ruthwell Cross. Papers from the Colloquium Sponsored by the Index of Christian Art, Princeton University, 8 December 1989*, ed. Brendan Cassidy (Princeton, N.J., 1992).

84. Briefly, some scholars believe that the Vercelli poem is an expansion of the text on the Ruthwell cross (Dickins and Ross); some argue that the Ruthwell poem is an abbreviation of the Vercelli text (Cook, Stanley); and some, often while holding one of the two opinions described, postulate an original poem or exemplar from which both poems were drawn (Dickins and Ross, Stanley). Until quite recently, the belief that roughly three hundred years separated sculpture and manuscript steered opinions towards the first of these positions. Now, there is considerable support for the view that the runic inscription was added sometime after the cross was sculpted and erected (e.g., Meyvaert, Page, and Stanley); the date of the Ruthwell poem may no longer be bound to the date of the sculpture. Eric Stanley suggests a late ninth-century date for the inscription, and reasons: "If the Vercelli poem was composed, say, fifty to a hundred years before the date of the manuscript in which it is preserved [late tenth century], a reasonable assumption, it need be no later than the date of the inscription" (396). Éamonn Ó Carragáin (1992) on the other hand, finds it "likely that the English verse . . . was part of the original design," (91).

See A. S. Cook, "Notes on the Ruthwell Cross," *PMLA* 17 (1902), 367–90; Bruce Dickins and Alan S. C. Ross, *The Dream of the Rood*, 4th ed. (London, 1954); Paul Meyvaert, "An Apocalypse Panel on the Ruthwell Cross," in Frank Tirro, ed., *Medieval and Renaissance Studies, Proceedings of the Southeastern Institute of Medieval and Renaissance Studies, Summer 1978* (Durham, N.C., 1982), pp. 3–32; Éamonn Ó Carragáin, "The Ruthwell Crucifixion Poem in Its Iconographic and Liturgical Contexts," *Peritia. Journal of the Medieval Academy of Ireland* 6–7 (1987–88), 1–71, and "Seeing, Reading, Singing the Ruthwell Cross: Vernacular Poetry, Old Roman Liturgy, Implied Audience," *Medieval Europe 1992, Prepublished Papers* VII, *Art and Symbolism*, pp. 91–96; R. I. Page, "Language and Dating in Old English Inscriptions," *Anglia* 77 (1959), 385–406, and *An Introduction to English Runes* (London, 1973); Eric G. Stanley, "The Ruthwell Cross Inscription: Some Linguistic and Literary Implications of Paul Meyvaert's paper, 'An Apocalypse Panel on the Ruthwell Cross,'" in his *A Collection of Papers with Emphasis on Old English Literature, Publications of the Dictionary of Old English*, vol. 3 (Toronto, 1987), pp. 384–99.

85. The condition of the Ruthwell Cross provides a manifestation of the fragmented, incomplete, indecipherable text. In 1642, the General Assembly of the Church of Scotland proclaimed the cross idolatrous and ordered that it be knocked down. Its parts were variously fractured, scattered, defaced, and buried; many are not recoverable because of loss or destruction. Some fragments lay for one hun-

dred and sixty years in the churchyard. Reverend Henry Duncan pieced the remains together in 1802; twenty-one years later he designed a cross-beam to replace
the lost original. In 1887, the reconstructed, supplemented cross was moved into
the church, its present site. There is considerable doubt, however, as to whether
the sculpture has been correctly reassembled and positioned. See Brendan Cassidy's recent volume, *The Ruthwell Cross*, for discussion of the cross's history,
present structure, and possible meaning.

86. At the time of its construction (ca. 700?), there were twenty figural
panels. The cross was severely damaged during the Reformation and only thirteen
of these have survived. See Brendan Cassidy, "The Later Life of the Ruthwell Cross:
From the Seventeenth Century to the Present" (3–34); Robert Farrell, "The Construction, Deconstruction, and Reconstruction of the Ruthwell Cross: Some Ca-
veats" (with Catherine Karkov; 35–47); and Paul Meyvaert, "A New Perspective on
the Ruthwell Cross" (95–166); all in Cassidy, ed., *The Ruthwell Cross*. Also see
Robert T. Farrell, "Reflections on the Iconography of the Ruthwell and Bewcastle
Crosses," in *Sources of Anglo-Saxon Culture*, ed. Paul E. Szarmach (Kalamazoo,
Mich., 1986), pp. 357–76.

87. Some have suggested that the depictions of the desert thematically represent a hermetic ideal. This, it is argued, would accord with the remote setting of
the sculpture. For example, Cassidy states: "The preponderance of desert allusions
and the choice of figures associated with the eremitic life suggested the monastic
milieu of the early Northumbrian church" ("The Later Life of the Ruthwell Cross,"
p. 31). See Farrell ("Reflections on the Iconography of the Ruthwell and Bewcastle
Crosses") for a summary of the problems of interpretation. There is a vast literature on this topic.

88. Seth Lerer's discussion of runes themselves as self-referential supports my
reading of the east and west sides of the cross: "Unlike the letters of a Christian world,
those of a pagan past derive their power from their own inscription. Runes, to put it
bluntly, are not 'symbols' of anything, but may instead be thought of as a power of
their own—a power activated by their proper cutting and inscription" (*Literacy and
Power in Anglo-Saxon England* [Lincoln, Neb., and London, 1991], pp. 16–17).

89. See Brian Stock ("Medieval Literacy, Linguistic Theory, and Social Organization," *New Literary History* 16:1 [1984], 13–29) and Stephen G. Nichols ("Introduction: Philology in a Manuscript Culture," *Speculum* 65:1 [1990], 1–10) for
discussions of the importance of texture and opacity to medieval texts and their
interpretation.

90. Ó Carragáin speculates about the relationships among the cross's pictorial
and verbal texts: "Poem and iconography explain and complement each other: the
poem presents Christ's victory on the Cross as a historical event which took place
on Good Friday; while the iconography presents the ways in which the Northumbrian church interpreted their liturgical participation in his victory . . ." ("The
Ruthwell Crucifixion Poem in its Iconographic and Liturgical Contexts," p. 50). See
also his "Seeing, Reading, and Singing the Ruthwell Cross."

91. The reader of the manuscript poem must imagine the absent speaker in a variety of roles and locations. Since the cross in its speech on the sculpture asks the reader to imagine it in a previous time and place, there is also a sense in which the reader's position in relation to *this* speaker is not literal.

92. "Christ over the Beasts and the Agnus Dei."

93. Michael Swanton, ed., *The Dream of the Rood* (Manchester, 1970), p. 13, n. 1. Also Sandra McEntire "The Devotional Context of the Cross Before A.D. 1000," p. 349; Robert T. Farrell, "Reflections of the Iconography of the Ruthwell and Bewcastle Crosses," p. 375, n. 6; Éamonn Ó Carragáin, "Christ over the Beasts and the Agnus Dei: Two Multivalent Panels on the Ruthwell and Bewcastle Crosses," p. 388; all in Paul E. Szarmach, ed., *Sources of Anglo-Saxon Culture* (Kalamazoo, Mich., 1986).

94. In a sensitive and imaginative reading of this panel on the Ruthwell and Bewcastle crosses, Éamonn Ó Carragáin discovers many meanings ranging from the explicit representation of Christ as judge to the association of the image with a canticle celebrating Christ's majesty in the heavens and his radiance—an association that would have been made by a monk completing lauds and seeing the sun rise behind the cross.

95. Ó Carragáin describes the spiritual significance of multivalence: "[Early medieval monks] are likely to have valued figural representations which were relevant to as many facets of their lives (individual and communal) as possible. . . . The concerns of an early medieval monastic patron are likely to have differed markedly from those of a modern scholar anxious to set forth a single coherent theme which can be abstracted from a series of figure-sculptures and to present that as the 'iconographic program' of the series" (378–79). "[In] monastic spirituality, one devotional perspective could coexist quite naturally with another, and indeed with several others. The primary artistic virtue of the monastic tradition was the ability to weave around any theme a rich web of spiritual associations. . . . Monastic writers like Bede seem to have rejoiced precisely in the variety of perspectives available to them at any one time" (398).

Irvine's observation regarding *The Dream of the Rood* suggests that the poem resembles the sculpture in its multiple significance: "As a sign [the cross] is capable of yielding several layers of meaning simultaneously, according to the principles for signification understood for typological events or objects in sacred history" ("Anglo-Saxon Literary Theory Exemplified in Old English Poems," p. 173).

Chapter 2

1. *Time and Narrative*, vol. 2, trans. Kathleen McLaughlin and David Pellauer, (Chicago, 1984), p. 99. In my understanding, configuration is the act of composition and refiguration that of interpretation.

2. In *Image on the Edge: The Margins of Medieval Art* (Cambridge, Mass., 1992), Michael Camille writes that "marginal art is about . . . the problem of

signifying nothing in order to give birth to meaning at the centre" (p. 48). He argues, though, that in the Gothic manuscripts he studies this avoidance of meaning is only a pretense creating a space for subversion.

3. *The Truth in Painting*, trans. Geoff Bennington and Ian McLeod (Chicago, 1987), p. 50.

4. Unfortunately, it was not feasible to reproduce the photographs in color in this publication.

5. The *Oxford English Dictionary* summarizes the history of the word's development: "The original senses of the Teutonic verb are those of taking or giving counsel, taking care or charge of a thing, having or exercising control over something, etc. These are also prominent in Old English, and the sense of 'advise' still survives as an archaism, usually distinguished from the prevailing sense of the word by the retention of the older spelling 'rede'. The sense of considering or explaining something obscure or mysterious is also common to the various languages, but the application of this to the interpretation of ordinary writing, and to the expression of this in speech, is confined to English and Old Norse (in the latter perhaps under English influence)."

6. This manuscript is thought to be contemporary with the Lindisfarne Gospels, and probably a product of the same scriptorium (Wilson, *Anglo-Saxon Art*, pp. 36 and 38).

7. "Some Attitudes Toward the Frame in Anglo-Saxon Manuscripts of the Tenth and Eleventh Centuries," *Artibus et Historiae*, Revista Internationale di Arti Visive e Cinema 5 (1982), 31–35. The Psalter was completed at Winchester in the second quarter of the tenth century.

8. "[C]IRCOS QUOQUE MULTOS IN HOC PRECEPIT FIERI LIBRO BENE COMPTOS COMPLETOS QUOQUE AGALMATIBUS VARIIS DECORATIS MULTIGENIS MINIIS PULCHRIS NECNON SIMUL AURO" (as reproduced in John Gage, "A Dissertation on St. Æthelwold's Benedictional," *Archaeologia* 24 [1832], 49). The dedication is translated and quoted in full by Francis Wormald in *The Benedictional of St. Æthelwold* (London, 1959).

9. "Replication and Depiction in Paleolithic Art," *Representations* 19 (Summer 1987), 111–47.

10. In the Echternach Gospels symbol page, there are two other meaningful compositional elements—the inscription, IMAGO LEONIS, and the parchment, a large proportion of which is unpainted. Waynes Dynes pays some attention to the lettering and more to the parchment, which he describes as "permeable," "compartmentalized," a signifier of "processed animal nature" ("Imago Leonis," *Gesta* 20:1 [1981], 35–41). Whitney Davis accounts for such an overlapping of semantic realms: "In a single pattern, several referential systems could be operating simultaneously: a notation may be commenting upon or labelling an image, an image may be an element in a heraldry, and so forth" (132).

11. An early eleventh-century manuscript, probably the product of a Canterbury scriptorium (Wilson, *Anglo-Saxon Art*, pp. 174 and 176).

12. This kind of visual interpretational play is a feature of much Anglo-Saxon art. The interlace of the Sutton Hoo belt buckle, for example, at first seems to be absolutely nonrepresentational, but then is discovered to be formed by the bodies of serpents. Foreground and background are easily misinterpreted when the Sutton Hoo shoulder clasps are first seen; when this mistake is corrected, the pattern of gold filigree that predominated is understood merely to fill the space between images of interlocking boars. (For illustrations see David M. Wilson, *Anglo-Saxon Art: From the Seventh Century to the Norman Conquest* [Woodstock, New York, 1984], figs. 6 and 7).

13. Davis intends his work to be applied to questions of interpretation generally, not just to the reading of paleolithic art. His article is primarily theoretical and methodological. He chooses paleolithic art as a "helpful test case" in a study of "a general problem, namely the context in which and the conventions by which a graphic pattern is taken to be a product of some reality" (111). I think, though, that his choice of an art that records chronological change reveals his adherence to the predominant belief in evolutionary development.

14. Ernst Kitzinger contrasts the ornamental carpet pages of Hiberno-Saxon manuscripts with "the book illumination of the South, where miniaturists never used ornament except to mark the beginning or the end of a chapter, or to frame an illustration." *Early Medieval Art*, revised ed. (Bloomington, Ind., 1983), p. 49.

15. Just before describing nonimage as the "possibility for . . . the decay" of the image, Davis says that "it is the unavoidable by-product of replicating the image." It is interesting to compare Derrida's interpretation of the dictionary definition of "parerga": "Dictionaries most often give 'hors-d'oeuvre', which is the strictest translation, but also 'accessory, foreign or secondary object', 'supplement', 'aside', 'remainder'. It is what the principal subject *must not become*" (*The Truth in Painting*, p. 54).

16. Although I have chosen to focus on manuscript illumination, frames in other forms of Anglo-Saxon art are equally complex and meaningful. The borders of the Bayeux Tapestry consist of patterns and images—vinescroll, human and animal figures, scenes from fables—that sometimes relate to the narrative of the "main" field, and sometimes seem oblivious to that portrayed action. The image in the frame may be part of the narrative, as when birds of prey in the upper border greedily observe the Battle of Hastings, or when warriors who have fallen in that battle lie in the border beneath the scene of conflict. The connection between the two is not always so explicit. Sometimes the scene in the border seems to be commenting on the other action; the peripheral figure of a naked man has been taken to signify the sexual nature of the relationship between a woman and man portrayed above, and the ships depicted in the border below the scene of Harold conversing with a messenger have been interpreted as representing either the content of the message or an omen in Harold's imagination. (See David M. Wilson, *The Bayeux Tapestry* [London, 1985] for a complete reproduction of the tapestry and a summary of critical works.) Whatever the content of the border, it is not

easily disregarded. The line of stitching that separates the main action from the border scenes is not treated as a firm division—there is frequent overlap. Inscription frames figural representation on four sides of the Franks Casket and on the north and south faces of the Ruthwell Cross; the ornamental carving on the cross's east and west sides is circumscribed with poetic text. The relationships between words, languages, script, images, and patterns, and the question of whether their positions are central or peripheral, invites careful study. These borders exemplify Anglo-Saxon frames that very literally must be read.

17. "Listen! I shall speak of the best of dreams, which came to me in the middle of the night, while other people (speech-bearers) slept." All quotations are from Krapp ed., The Vercelli Book, ASPR, vol. 2.

18. Seth Lerer's chapter, "Poet of the *Boceras*: Literacy and Power in the Old English *Daniel*" (*Literacy and Power in Anglo-Saxon Literature* [Lincoln, Neb., and London, 1991], pp. 126–57) offers a reading of this poem that parallels my own in its concern with structure and interpretation. As I do, Lerer understands *Daniel* to be a poem about writing and reading, and specifically about the difficulty of interpreting elusive texts. He places *Daniel*'s interpretive concerns within a context of scriptural exposition as practiced through the tradition of Latin monastic learning, and particularly as discussed by Aldhelm in *De Virginitate*'s reference to the Book of Daniel. Lerer's reading of the poem is effectively argued, although the hermeneutical ideology he rehearses still presents a text controlled by the author and ultimately conquered by the reader (despite a stated attempt to celebrate confusion, [127]).

19. All quotations from *Daniel* follow G. P. Krapp, ed., The Junius Manuscript, ASPR 1 (New York, 1931).

20. Our reading, then, differs from the reading of Nebuchadnezzar. In *The Dream of the Rood*, both the cross and the dreamer are model readers. They contextualize the cross's story, placing it within an interpretive framework. The interpretation in *Daniel* is not performed by the king; he does not "comprehend" his dream, so he cannot link it to his life. Daniel's interpretation of the first dream is not given in the poem.

21. The temporal situation of the dreams is comparable to that of the narrative "digressions" in *Beowulf*, as described below.

22. "Until the almighty lord out of necessity set him lower, as he does to many who rise up because of excessive pride."

23. *The Larger Rhetorical Patterns in Anglo-Saxon Poetry* (New York, 1935), p. 72.

24. *Reading Frames in Modern Fiction* (Princeton, N.J., 1985), p. 6.

25. "Then Azarias, the holy, sang out through the burning flame in thanksgiving; eager for great deeds he suffered, praised the lord."

26. The event of the writing on the wall is also given a spatial frame. Before its occurrence, the physical setting of the miracle is sketched in: "Him þæt tacen wearð þær he to starude" ("the sign was made for him, before his eyes," 717). After the angel's act of writing on the wall has been described, the account is immediately repeated in such a way that the event is placed, again, as an object of the king's perception: "Geseah he engles hand / in sele writan Sennera wite" ("he saw the angel's hand in the hall writing of the affliction of the Shinarites," 725b–26). The scope of the king's vision constitutes a physical context for the miracle.

27. The miracle of the salvation of the three children is also referred to in these words: "Swa wordum spræc werodes ræswa, / Babilone weard, siððan he beacen onget, / swutol tacen godes (486–88a); "Thus the counsellor of the people, the guardian of Babylon, said with words, after he understood the symbol, the clear sign of God.") Both miracles occur because of the intervention of an angel. An event whose cause is external to the narrative, and which therefore is incoherent in relation to the fictional world, must be connected to that world through understanding.

28. Lerer also discusses the significance of the angel's message as specifically a written text, arguing that "run" in line 740 has assumed the meaning of "runic inscription" (141–43). In my reading, the two meanings—mystery and inscription—converge at this point.

29. "The dreadful sign was made for him before his eyes, in front of the noblemen, within the hall."
"Then the angel of the lord caused his hand to come there, as a monstrous thing, into that hall."
"He saw the angel's hand in the hall writing of the affliction of the Shinarites."

30. Many scholars have thought *Daniel* to be incomplete. A modern expectation of narrative closure has probably contributed to the belief that the poem as we have it must be lacking its original conclusion. See, for example, G. P. Krapp, The Junius Manuscript, ASPR, vol. 1 (New York, 1931), p. xxxi, and Stanley Greenfield, *A Critical History of Old English Literature* (New York, 1965), p. 160. Recently, critical attitudes have shifted to accommodate *Daniel's* limitations and abrupt conclusion. See R. T. Farrell, ed., *Daniel and Azarias* (London, 1974), p. 6, and Stanley Greenfield and Daniel Calder, *A New Critical History of Old English Literature* (New York, 1986), pp. 217–18.

31. Frames are formative of structure and have, therefore, been a focus of deconstructive theory. Alan Kennedy says that "the whole deconstructive process can be thought of as a meditation on borders" ("The Thinking of Criticism," *University of Toronto Quarterly* 56 (1987), 444). Derrida associates frames with building materials when he speaks of their inevitable shifting: "The frame labors [*travaille*] indeed. Place of labor, structurally bordered origin of surplus value, i.e., overflowed [*débordée*] on these two borders by what it overflows, it gives [*travaille*] indeed. Like wood. It creaks and cracks, breaks down and dislocates even as it cooperates in the production of the product, overflows it and is deduc(t)ed from it. It never lets itself be simply exposed"

(*The Truth in Painting*, p. 75). Frames are essential and hidden, like the wooden framework of a house (and, following from deconstruction's roots in psychoanalysis, like the unconscious).

32. "Teach yourself by him, understand virtue; I, wise in winters, told this story about you." All quotations are from Fr. Klaeber, ed., *Beowulf and the Fight at Finnsburg*, 3rd ed. (Boston, 1950).

33. *The Yale Journal of Criticism: Interpretation in the Humanities* 1 (1987), 21–38. Although Brooks speaks of nineteenth-century novels, the structure he describes is comparable to that of *Beowulf*.

34. "There was song and music both together before Healfdene's leader in battle, the harp [wood of joy] was touched, a tale often told, when Hroðgar's scop was to utter entertainment in the hall at the mead bench, about Finn's retainers, when disaster came upon them . . ."

35. "The lay was sung, the singer's tale. Joy again ascended, bench-noise brightened, cupbearers presented wine from wonderful vessels."

36. *The Heroic Age* (Cambridge, 1912), pp. 1–2.

37. pp. xii–xiii.

38. *The Digressions in Beowulf*, Medium Aevum Monographs. (Oxford, 1950).

39. "Contiguity and Similarity in the Beowulf Digressions," *Medieval Studies Conference*, Frankfurt and New York, 1983, ed. Bald and Weinstock, pp. 71–83.

40. "The Narrative Art of Beowulf," in *Medieval Narrative: A Symposium*, ed. Hans Bekker-Nielsen et al. (Odense, 1979), p. 64; rpt. in Stanley's *A Collection of Papers with Emphasis on Old English Literature*, Publications of the Dictionary of Old English 3 (Toronto, 1987), pp. 170–91.

41. Diller attributes this voice to the author (p. 72).

42. *Narratology: Introduction to the Theory of Narrative*, trans. Christine van Boheemen (Toronto, 1985), p. 143.

43. See Stanley, pp. 59–60.

44. See chapter 1 on the question of identity in Old English poetry.

45. *The Larger Rhetorical Patterns . . .* , p. 7.

46. "The Interlace Structure of Beowulf," *University of Toronto Quarterly* 37 (1967), 1–17.

47. "Imago Leonis," p. 38.

48. Derrida (*The Truth in Painting*) says of the "parergon" (which he describes as "an accessory that one is obliged to welcome on the border" [54], "an activity or operation which comes beside" [56], something "exceptional" [58]):

"With respect to the work which can serve as a ground for it, it merges into the wall, and then, gradually, into the general text. With respect to the background which the general text is, it merges into the work which stands out against the general background" p. 61).

49. *Reading Frames* . . . , p. 21.

50. *The Truth in Painting*, p. 63.

51. In *The Larger Rhetorical Patterns* . . .

52. "A moth ate words. That seemed to me a strange event when I heard of that wonder, that the worm had consumed someone's poem, a thief in the darkness [had swallowed] the glorious saying and its strong foundation. The thievish guest was not at all the wiser although he swallowed the words." Quotation is from Krapp and Dobbie, eds., The Exeter Book, ASPR, vol. 3.

53. "The Rhetoric of the Exeter Book Riddles," *Speculum* 49 (1974), 439.

54. I refer here to Fred Robinson's article "Artful Ambiguities in the Old English 'Book-Moth' Riddle," *Anglo-Saxon Poetry: Essays in Appreciation*, ed. L. E. Nicholson and D. W. Frese, (Notre Dame, Ind., 1975), pp. 355–62.

55. *The Dialogic Imagination: Four Essays*, ed. Michael Holquist, trans. Caryl Emerson and Michael Holquist (Austin, Texas, 1981), p. 49.

56. Language that refers to itself, placing itself in a context, does not actually constitute a border, but says that a border exists. It speaks about itself from a certain distance—from across the border, showing that there is a limit, a shape, to what has been said.

57. Brian Stock ("Medieval Literacy, Linguistic Theory, and Social Organization," *New Literary History* 16:1 [1984], 13–29) and Stephen G. Nichols ("Introduction: Philology in a Manuscript Culture," *Speculum* 65:1 [1990], 1–10) discuss the foregrounding of texture (and therefore opacity) in medieval textual traditions.

58. "For the [artistic] prose writer, the object is a focal point for heteroglot voices among which his own voice must also sound; these voices create the background necessary for his own voice, outside of which his artistic prose nuances cannot be perceived, and without which they 'do not sound'" (278).

59. In a paper delivered at the 1988 International Congress on Medieval Studies, Glory Dharmaraj spoke of the coincidence of Christian and pagan voices in *Beowulf*; each language is seen to be limited, or bounded, in relation to the other ("*Beowulf* and Bakhtin: A Study in the Interplay of Voices," Western Michigan University, Kalamazoo, Mich., 7 May 1988).

My topic in chapter 3 is the way the compositional structure of Old English poetry—and sometimes its subject matter as well—brings about a merging of past and present; a "dialogue," in the Bakhtinian sense, results from this contact (just as it does from the overlap of contemporaneous cultures).

60. *Speculum* 47 (1972), 207–26.

61. Gerard Genette, "Modern Mimology: The Dream of a Poetic Language," trans. Thais E. Morgan, *PMLA* 104 (1989), 212.

62. See Broderick, pp. 31–35.

Chapter 3

1. See Helmut Gneuss, "The Origin of Standard Old English and Æthelwold's School at Winchester," *Anglo-Saxon England* (1972), vol. 1, pp. 63–83.

2. Michael Lapidge and Michael Winterbottom, ed. and trans., *Wulfstan of Winchester: Life of St. Æthelwold* (Oxford, 1991).

3. J. Zupitza, ed., *Ælfrics Grammatik und Glossar* (Berlin, 1880; rpt., with preface by Helmut Gneuss, Berlin, 1966).

4. John Miles Foley provides a detailed study of the significance of these traces in his *The Singer of Tales in Performance* (Bloomington, Ind., 1995). He writes that "traditional oral forms persist in manuscripts not because they are merely useful or charming, or metrically or stylistically correct, but because they continue to encode an immanent context, a referential background that deepens and complicates whatever more particular events occupy the foreground in a given work" (183).

5. Since Francis P. Magoun, following Milman Parry and Albert Lord, made the argument that Old English poetry belongs absolutely to the category "oral-formulaic," the issue has occupied a central place in Old English literary studies. Recently, Katherine O'Brien O'Keeffe has demonstrated that the two modes of transmission do not exist as pure states in Old English verse, but that "formulaic thinking" was both oral and written. This assertion also draws into question the validity of source hunting, since similarities between two texts do not lead to the conclusion that one was the source for the other; she argues that the method of source hunting "presupposes our own literate ideology." Memory functioned differently in a transitional literary culture, and questions of the poetry's oral or written character, or of the influence of one text upon another, must be reconceptualized. (Francis P. Magoun, "Oral-Formulaic Character of Anglo-Saxon Narrative Poetry," *Speculum* 28 [1953], 446–67; Katherine O'Brien O'Keeffe, "Orality and the Developing Text of *Cædmon's Hymn*," in her *Visible Song: Transitional Literacy in Old English Verse* [Cambridge, 1990], pp. 23–46, and "The Written Remembered: Residual Orality and the Question of Sources," Twenty-third International Congress on Medieval Studies, Western Michigan University, Kalamazoo, Mich., 6 May 1988.)

6. *A Key to Old Poems*, p. 80.

7. "The Desire for Origins: An Archaeology of Anglo-Saxon Studies," *Style* 20:2 (1986), 142–56. Frantzen considers further this impulse in Anglo-Saxon scholarship in *Desire for Origins . . .* , pp. 83–95.

8. "The Text and the Voice," *New Literary History* 16:1 (1984), 78. This is an exciting article, crucial to the understanding of the implications of orality for written medieval poetry.

9. See, for example, Ruth Finnegan, *Literacy and Orality: Studies in the Technology of Communication* (Oxford, 1988); John Miles Foley, *Traditional Oral Epic: The Odyssey, Beowulf, and the Serbo-Croatian Return Song* (Berkeley, Calif., 1990), *Immanent Art: From Structure to Meaning in Traditional Oral Epic* (Bloomington, Ind., 1991), and *The Singer of Tales in Performance* (Bloomington, Ind., 1995); Walter Ong, *Orality and Literacy: The Technologizing of the Word* (London, 1982); Jeff Opland, *Anglo-Saxon Oral Poetry* (New Haven, Conn., 1980); Alain Renoir, *A Key to Old Poems: The Oral-Formulaic Approach to the Interpretation of West-Germanic Verse* (University Park, Pa., 1988); and Paul Zumthor, *Oral Poetry: An Introduction*, trans. Kathryn Murphy-Judy (Minneapolis, 1990), originally published as *Introduction à la poésie orale* (Paris, 1983).

10. A partial list of important works on this topic includes: Franz H. Bäuml, "Varieties and Consequences of Medieval Literacy and Illiteracy," *Speculum* 55 (1980), 237–65; Rosamund McKitterick, *The Carolingians and the Written Word* (Cambridge, 1989) and *The Uses of Literacy in Early Modern Europe* (Cambridge, 1990); Katherine O'Brien O'Keeffe, *Visible Song: Transitional Literacy in Old English Verse* (Cambridge, 1990); M. B. Parkes, "The Literacy of the Laity," in *The Medieval World*, ed. David Daiches and Anthony Thorlby (London, 1973), pp. 555–77 (vol. 2 of *Literature and Western Civilization*); and Brian Stock, *The Implications of Literacy: Written Language and Models of Interpretation in the Eleventh and Twelfth Centuries* (Princeton, N.J., 1983) and "Medieval Literacy, Linguistic Theory, and Social Organization," *New Literary History* 16:1 (1984), 13–29.

11. *The Implications of Literacy*, p. 9.

12. For a different opinion see Norman E. Eliason, "The 'Improvised Lay' in *Beowulf*" (*Philological Quarterly* 31 [April, 1952], 171–79), who argues that too many assumptions have been made about this passage. He proposes as a translation of lines 870b–72, "he recalled [or, spoke] more words, linked to truth; the man once again skillfully brought into notice Beowulf's feat . . ."; "wordum wrixlan" (874a) he reads simply as "to exchange words," i.e., "to speak." In this way, Eliason takes away from the most crucial elements of the description any reference to oral composition.

13. Quotations are from Klaeber, ed., *Beowulf and The Fight at Finnsburg*.

14. Drawing on the work of Parry, Lord, and Magoun, Alain Renoir in *A Key to Old Poems* offers an "account of the theory of oral-formulaic composition": "In its barest outline, the theory argues that the fully trained oral-formulaic poet comes equipped with a stock of extremely flexible paradigms functioning at essentially three different but mutually supportive levels of composition to enable him or her to produce on the spot poems of various lengths with a controlled structure:

(1) metrical and grammatical paradigms . . . ; (2) themes which act as paradigms for all types of situations . . . ; and (3) larger traditional topics" (54–55).

15. Otto Jespersen defines three methods by means of which such vocabulary development could occur: by "affixing native endings to foreign words" (his examples include "biscopsetl" ["episcopal see"] and "scriftscir" ["parish confessor's district"]); by giving an existing word a new sense (such as "god" and "witega" [at first "wise man," later also "prophet"]); by building new words out of old ones ("tungolwitegan" ["star prophets," i.e., the Magi] and "ansetla" ["sole settler" or "hermit"]). *Growth and Structure of the English Language*, 10th ed. (Oxford, 1982), pp. 39–42.

16. Foley speaks of the poetry's "extratextual resonance" which "bring[s] the immanence of tradition to the individual text and individual moment" (153). ("Texts That Speak to Readers Who Hear: Old English Poetry and the Languages of Oral Tradition," in Allen Frantzen, ed., *Speaking Two Languages*, pp. 141–56.)

17. "Generative Composition in Beowulf," *English Studies* 58 (1977), 201.

18. *The Savage Mind* (Chicago, 1966), pp. 17–18.

19. Gillian Overing also refers to the concept of bricolage in her reading of *Beowulf*, applying it to her own interpretive work in order to emphasize the "experimental nature" of her interpretation, its relationship to what has already been said about the poem, and its open-endedness. In my opinion, this method of reading *Beowulf* appropriately follows the poem's own bricolage-like construction; she aligns her own hermeneutics with that of the poem. (*Language, Sign, and Gender in Beowulf*, p. xiv.)

20. Quotations from *Andreas* follow Krapp, ed., The Vercelli Book, ASPR 2; quotation from *Juliana* follows Krapp and Dobbie, eds., The Exeter Book, ASPR 3.

21. Quotations from *The Phoenix*, *Christ II*, and *Guthlac B* follow Krapp and Dobbie, eds., The Exeter Book, ASPR 3; quotation from *Elene* follows Krapp, ed., The Vercelli Book, ASPR 2.

22. The compositional similarities between the "coining of compounds" and the "use of formulas and themes" is discussed by Greenfield and Calder (*A New Critical History of Old English Literature* [New York, 1986], pp. 126–27).

23. Important articles include Stanley B. Greenfield, "The Formulaic Expression of the Theme of 'Exile' in Anglo-Saxon Poetry," *Speculum* 30 (1955), 200–206 (rpt. in J. B. Bessinger, Jr., and S. J. Kahrl, eds., *Essential Articles for the Study of Old English Poetry* [Hamden, Conn., 1968], pp. 352–62); Adrien Bonjour, "Beowulf and the Beasts of Battle," *PMLA* 72 (1957), 563–73; David K. Crowne, "The Hero on the Beach: An Example of Composition by Theme in Anglo-Saxon Poetry," *Neuphilologische Mitteilungen* 61 (1960), 362–72; and Alain Renoir, "Old English Formulas and Themes as Tools for Contextual Interpretation," in *Modes of Inter-*

pretation in Old English Literature, ed. Phyllis R. Brown, Georgia R. Crampton, and Fred C. Robinson (Toronto, 1986), pp. 65–79.

Foley includes resonant, repeated themes among the vestiges of oral-traditional composition that he studies in Homeric and Old English written texts. See, for example, his chapter, "Indexed Translation: The Poet's Self-Interruption in the Old English *Andreas*" in *The Singer of Tales in Performance*, pp. 181–207.

24. "Text and Voice," p. 83.

25. Renoir is especially concerned, in "Old English Formulas and Themes . . ." and *A Key to Old Poems*, with this interpretation of formulas and contexts in our present-day reading of Old English poetry, comparing our understanding to that of an Anglo-Saxon audience. He describes the details of the reader's active participation in the composition of the poem, based on his or her previous knowledge of formulaic sequences and on the interplay between anticipation and omission (or "semantic gapping"). See "Oral-Formulaic Context and Critical Interpretation: General Principles" (pp. 81–104) and "Oral-Formulaic Context in *Beowulf*: The Hero on the Beach and the Grendel Episode" (pp. 107–32) in *A Key to Old Poems*.

26. In his consideration of the reception of Old English poetry—inscribed, as it is, with oral-traditional idiom—Foley proposes that "each [member of the audience] brings to the process of interpretation a deep knowledge of how to 'read' the text before him or her, of how to construe the traditional signals in their full metonymic, inherent meaning" ("Texts That Speak to Readers Who Hear," p. 150). Elsewhere, Foley writes, "When we 'read' or interpret any traditional performance or text with attention to the metonymic meaning it necessarily summons, we are, in effect, recontextualizing that work, bridging Iserian 'gaps of indeterminacy' . . . reaffirming contiguity with other performances or texts, or, better, with the ever-immanent tradition itself." ("Orality, Textuality, Interpretation," in A. N. Doane and Carol Braun Pasternack, eds., *Vox Intexta: Orality and Textuality in the Middle Ages* [Madison, Wisc., 1991], p. 43.)

27. The association could just as easily follow the other direction, so that the depiction of the Christian Lord's benevolence would be applied to a secular ruler in order to make him (and the whole notion of monarchy) more attractive.

28. " . . . from when the sun glided upwards in the morning, the glorious star, over the lands, the bright candle of God, the eternal lord. . . ." Quotation from E. Van K. Dobbie, ed., The Anglo-Saxon Minor Poems, ASPR 6 (New York, 1942).

29. "Introduction to the Structural Analysis of Narratives," in his *Image, Music, Text*, pp. 79–124.

30. "On meeting in 'life', it is most unlikely that the invitation to take a seat would not immediately be followed by the act of sitting down; in narrative these two units, contiguous from a mimetic point of view, may be separated by a long series of insertions . . ." (119).

31. To describe certain moments as "cardinal," "crucial," or "essential" is to endow them with a priority in relation to other aspects of the poem. I discuss the presumptions involved in such categorization in chapter 2. For my present purposes, I mean only to articulate their importance to a poem's narrative thread, not to suggest that they have exceptional significance to the poem as a whole.

32. In Lewis's interpretation, "the tiny animals proclaim that the Incarnate Logos and salvation through his crucufixion extend throughout creation" (144); a close study of the stories suggested by the animals (read in light of Christian doctrine, Isidorian etymology, and Insular legend) leads her to the conclusion that each is a "Christological image" preoccupied "with food and nourishment," and therefore serving "as a stunning metaphor for the Eucharist" (151). ("Sacred Calligraphy: The Chi Rho Page in the Book of Kells," *Traditio* 36 [1980], 139–59.)

Jackson J. Campbell, in his consideration of the style of Anglo-Saxon painting, equates its abstraction with spirituality: "[The] laws of aesthetic creation (of Anglo-Saxon artists] . . . require a complex process of cerebration coupled with emotional reaction, using only small amounts of existential reality to lead the minds and the reactions of the viewers to truer and more meaningful spiritual reality" (35). ("Some Aspects of Meaning in Anglo-Saxon Art and Literature," *Annuals Mediaevale* 15 [1974], 5–45.) This description subverts our notions of narrative. The figural and linear decoration of the Chi Rho page would be read as "cardinal functions" directed toward a primary spiritual signification and supported by the representational letters.

Lewis and Campbell give much attention to the significance of style. Both, however, attempt to recuperate abstraction into the forward movement of signification, thereby making it more easily comprehendible.

33. Originally, there were more illuminated pages; probably fifteen have been lost.

34. *Beowulf and the Fight at Finnsburg*, pp. lvii and lii, respectively.

35. In chapter 2, I consider the *Beowulf* digressions with regard to framing structures in Old English poetry.

36. The layout of the poems on the manuscript page, as well as the predominance of deviations in their narrative structure, may be an aspect of such a representation. Katherine O'Brien O'Keeffe, in tracing the manuscript history of *Cædmon's Hymn* ("Orality and the Developing Text of *Cædmon's Hymn*"), has found that, whereas lineation and pointing are quite consistent between copies of the Latin translation of the *Hymn*, "the Old English *Hymn* . . . is never displayed graphically by metrical line, nor does punctuation distinguish lines or half-lines or act consistently as a marker of grammatical divisions" (46). She relates the spatialization of a text to literacy, and equates the lack of regular spacing in the transciption of the Old English poem to its continuing oral quality. Perhaps this connection between lack of spatialization and orality also embraces the narrative structure

of the poetry and, therefore, its depiction of time. Writing introduces a graphic and a narrative linearity; the irregular *"mise-en-page"* (O'Keeffe) of Old English poetry may correspond to its discontinuous narrative.

See Suzanne Fleischman, "The Discourse of the Medieval Text," pp. 34–35, for a discussion of the significance of repetition in literatures with "strong oral storytelling traditions."

37. "Replication and Depiction in Paleolithic Art."

38. Allen Frantzen's paper "The Archaeology of Deconstruction and the Study of Medieval Sources" ("New Approaches in Medieval Studies," Centre for Medieval Studies, Toronto, 29 October 1988) has been very influential in my thinking about Bede's account of Cædmon. He argues that many of the binary oppositions that we perceive in "Anglo-Saxon cultural and literary history" ("the triumph of Christianity over pagan cultures; textuality—as defined by the rules used to study written texts—preferred to orality; the transformation of Latin into vernacular literature; and the conversion of native [pagan] narrative subjects to Christian themes") are represented in the *Ecclesiastical History* (11).

Since delivering this paper, Frantzen has published a more extensive critique of Bede's story of Cædmon (*Desire for Origins . . .* [New Brunswick, N.J., and London, 1990], pp. 134–67) in which he reads the text as suppressing "coercion" and "conflict," and "silenc[ing] Cædmon and his resistance" (141–42).

Seth Lerer also rereads Bede's *Cædmon* and recognizes it as ideologically interested (*Literacy and Power . . .* [Lincoln, Neb., and London, 1991], pp. 23, 33–35, and 42–48). He speaks of Bede as "transforming" the old secular values and customs into the new and Christian, creating a text which "argue[s] . . . for the institutional authority of the Roman Church and its rites *and* for the literary authority of Bede's own narrative persona" (47–48)

39. "Orality and the Developing Text of *Caedmon's Hymn*".

40. Allen Frantzen suggests that perhaps "the vernacular was created as a paraphrase of the Latin" (*Desire for Origins . . .* , p. 146). If this is the case, the Old English loses its priority, and the gloss becomes a translation rather than a record.

41. O'Keeffe is using the term "variation" to describe the writer's alteration of a formulaic half-line, not to describe the poetic technique to which I have been referring as "variation." In my understanding, a formulaic half-line can be either an exact repetition of a verse that occurs throughout Old English poetry or a modification of a verse, retaining its grammatical and rhythmic structure. "Variation" usually refers to the restatement of an idea (often) within a passage of poetry; it may or may not correspond with the first statement in its linguistic structure.

42. Meyer Schapiro, writing on the topic of the semiotics of a painting's frame and field, considers the cavepainter's response to a previous image ("On Some Problems in the Semiotics of Visual Art: Field and Vehicle in Image-Signs," *Semiotica* 1 [1969], 223–42). The painter did not preserve that image and seek a clean

surface for a new drawing but, in fact, seems to have deliberately returned to the place that had already been used. The cavepainter, Schapiro speculates, may have "thought of his own work . . . as occupying on the wall a place reserved for successive paintings because of a special rite or custom, as one makes fires year after year on the same hearth over past embers . . ." (223). The surface, perhaps, was special because of its memories and associations; the connotations deriving from its previous use were valued.

43. O'Keeffe, p. 41.

44. "The Archaeology of Deconstruction . . .," p. 12.

45. Alain Renoir suggests the possibility that "what we call Caedmon's *Hymn* is in fact a retranslation of Bede's own translation into Latin of the Old English poem which Caedmon had supposedly composed orally some seventy years earlier" (*A Key to Old Poems*, p. 80).

46. Allen Frantzen writes that the text "silences Cædmon" and allows him only to "[sing] in Bede's voice" (*Desire for Origins* . . . , p. 142). But the Latin text, he continues, was never complete in itself—it needed, as a supplement, the Old English gloss (143). In my reading, it is through this gloss and subsequent rereadings (rewritings) that Cædmon is given back his voice—although his "speech" is never direct or univocal.

47. *The Dialogic Imagination*, p. 76. Bakhtin is speaking here of parody as the predecessor and model for the novel, but the relationship between the two languages is similar to that between Latin and Old English in translations and glosses of the *Hymn*. In parody—which is an "intentional stylistic hybrid" (76)— one language or style of language is seen "against the background" of another (75). In his metaphor of a dialogue, each language or style is cast as a speaking subject.

48. Bakhtin, p. 174.

49. Trans. Joyce Marshall (Toronto, 1976).

50. "I was by the bank, near the seawall, at the shore; I remained fixed in my first location. There were few people who beheld my dwelling place there in solitude, but each morning the shining wave played around me with a watery embrace. Little did I think that I sooner or later should ever speak, mouthless, over the meadbench, exchange words. That is something of a wonder, curious to the mind of one who does not know these things, how the point of a knife and the right hand—someone's intention and the point together—pressed me for this purpose, that I should boldly announce a message to you, for us two alone, so that other people would not relate our words further." Quotation is from Krapp and Dobbie., eds., The Exeter Book, ASPR 3, riddle No. 60.

51. *Neophilologus* 62 (1978), 609–15.

52. This riddle (No. 47 in ASPR 3) is quoted in full in chapter 2.

53. "Artful Ambiguities in the Old English 'Book-Moth' Riddle," *Anglo-Saxon Poetry: Essays in Aprreciation*, ed., L. E. Nicholson and D. W. Frese (Notre Dame, Ind., 1975), pp. 355–62.

54. Seth Lerer, in his chapter "The Riddle and the Book" (*Literacy and Power* . . . , pp. 97–125) discusses Old English riddles that concern different aspects and implications of the craft of writing.

55. I refer here to Roberta Frank's article "Some Uses of Paronomasia in Old English Scriptural Verse" (*Speculum* 47 [1972], 207–26), which I discuss in chapter 2 in regard to framed language.

56. *Daniel and Azarias* (London, 1974), p. 139.

57. *Speculum* 55 (1980), 237–65.

58. See note 23 above.

59. The structures and attitudes described by Bäuml as existing in medieval texts resemble those found by Bakhtin in the novel. Bakhtin says of prenovelistic discourse, with specific reference to parody, "Every word used 'with conditions attached', every word enclosed in intonational quotation marks, is likewise an intentional hybrid—if only because the speaker insulates himself from this word as if from another 'language', as if from a style" (*The Dialogic Imagination*, p. 76).

60. *Truth and Method*, pp. 273–74.

Afterword

1. "Here one may still see their footprints, but we cannot follow after them; therefore we have now lost both the wealth and the wisdom, because we did not want to bend our minds to that track." Quotation follows Henry Sweet, ed., *King Alfred's West-Saxon Version of Gregory's* Pastoral Care, vol. 1, Early English Text Society 45 (London 1871–72), p. 4.

2. " . . . and often a quill made a track on me, over my dark surface, with useful drops, swallowed dye, a part of the stream, stepped on me again, traveled a dark path." Quotation is from Krapp and Dobbie, eds., The Exeter Book, ASPR, vol. 3.

3. *A Poetics of Postmodernism* (New York, 1988), p. xi.

4. I take this term from Catherine Belsey: "Expressive realism belongs roughly to the last century and a half, the period of industrial capitalism. . . . The Aristotelian concept of art as mimesis, the imitation of reality, was widely current throughout the Renaissance and particularly during the eighteenth century. Expressive realism was the product of a fusion of this concept with the new Romantic conviction that poetry, as 'the spontaneous overflow of powerful feelings', expressed the perceptions and emotions of a person 'possessed of more than usual organic sensibility' (Wordsworth)." *Critical Practice*, pp. 7–8.

5. Fred C. Robinson's *Beowulf and the Appositive Style* (Knoxville, Tenn., 1985) also insists upon the relevance of this interaction. Finding the principle of apposition at work in compounds, variation, and narrative structure, Robinson argues that apposition is not simply a poetic convention but a way of expressing ideas in order to elicit an appropriate interpretive response. Ultimately, the Christian and pagan elements of the poem are left in apposition, their relationship free of any overt, explanatory connectives.

Bibliography

Primary Sources

Colgrave, B., and R. A. B. Mynors, eds. *Bede's Ecclesiastical History of the English People*. Oxford: Clarendon Press, 1969.

Dobbie, E. Van K., ed. *The Anglo-Saxon Minor Poems*. Anglo-Saxon Poetic Records 6. New York: Columbia University Press, 1942. Hereafter abbreviated as ASPR.

Lapidge, Michael, and Michael Winterbottom, ed. and trans. *Wulfstan of Winchester: Life of St. Æthelwold*. Oxford: Oxford University Press, 1991.

Gollancz, Israel, ed. *The Cædmon Manuscript of Anglo-Saxon Biblical Poetry*. Oxford: Oxford University Press, 1927.

Klaeber, Fr., ed. *Beowulf and the Fight at Finnsburg*, 3rd ed. Boston: D. C. Heath and Co., 1950.

Krapp, G. P., ed. *The Junius Manuscript*. ASPR 1. New York: Columbia University Press, 1931.

———. *The Vercelli Book*. ASPR 2. New York: Columbia University Press, 1932.

Krapp, G. P., and E. Van K. Dobbie, eds. *The Exeter Book*. ASPR 3. New York: Columbia University Press, 1936.

Sweet, Henry, ed. *King Alfred's West-Saxon Version of Gregory's Pastoral Care*. Part I. Early English Text Society 45. London, 1871–72.

Whitelock, Dorothy, ed. *Sweet's Anglo-Saxon Reader*, 15th ed. Oxford: Clarendon Press, 1967.

Zupitza, J., ed. *Ælfrics Grammatik und Glossar*. Berlin: Weidmann, 1880; rpt., with preface by Helmut Gneuss, Berlin: Weidmann, 1966.

151

Secondary Sources

Bakhtin, Mikhail. *The Dialogic Imagination: Four Essays*. Trans. Caryl Emerson and Michael Holquist. Ed. Michael Holquist. Austin, Texas: University of Texas Press, 1981.

Bal, Mieke. *Narratology: Introduction to the Theory of Narrative*. Trans. Christine van Boheemen. Toronto: University of Toronto Press, 1985.

Barthes, Roland. "The Death of the Author." In his *Image, Music, Text*. Trans. and ed. Stephen Heath. New York: Hill and Wang, 1977, pp. 142–48.

——. "Diderot, Brecht, Eisenstein." *Image, Music, Text*, pp. 69–78.

——. "From Work to Text." *Image, Music, Text*, pp. 155–64.

——. "Introduction to the Structural Analysis of Narratives." *Image, Music, Text*, pp. 79–124.

Bartlett, Adeline C. *The Larger Rhetorical Patterns in Anglo-Saxon Poetry*. New York: Columbia University Press, 1935; rpr. AMS Press, 1966.

Bäuml, Franz. "Varieties and Consequences of Medieval Literacy and Illiteracy." *Speculum* 55 (1980), 237–65.

Behler, Ernst. "Deconstruction versus Hermeneutics: Derrida and Gadamer on Text and Interpretation." *Southern Humanities Review* 21:3 (1987), 201–23

Belsey, Catherine. *Critical Practice*. London: Methuen, 1980.

Benjamin, Walter. "The Storyteller: Reflections on the Works of Nikolai Leskov." In his *Illuminations: Essays and Reflections*. Trans. Harry Zohn. Ed. Hannah Arendt. New York: Schocken Books, 1969.

Benveniste, Emile. *Problems in General Linguistics*. Coral Gables: University of Miami Press, 1971.

Bonjour, Adrien. "*Beowulf* and the Beasts of Battle." *PMLA* 72 (1957), 563–73.

——. *The Digressions in Beowulf*. Medium Aevum Monographs, vol. 5. Oxford: Blackwell, 1950.

Bosworth, Joseph, and T. Northcote Toller, eds. *An Anglo-Saxon Dictionary*. Oxford, Oxford University Press 1882. With a *Supplement* by Toller. Oxford: Clarendon Press, 1921. *Revised and Enlarged Addenda* by Alistair Campbell. Oxford: Clarendon Press, 1972.

Bragg, Lois. *The Lyric Speakers of Old English Poetry*. Rutherford, Madison, Teaneck, N.J.: Fairleigh Dickinson University Press, 1991.

Broderick, H. R. "Some Attitudes Toward the Frame in Anglo-Saxon Manuscripts of the Tenth and Eleventh Centuries." *Artibus et Historiae. Revista Internationale di Arti Visive e Cinema* 5 (1982), 31–35.

Brooks, Peter. "The Storyteller." *The Yale Journal of Criticism: Interpretation in the Humanities* 1 (1987), 21– 38.

Bryson, Norman. *Vision and Painting: The Logic of the Gaze*. London: The Mac-Millan Press, 1983.

Camille, Michael. *Image on the Edge: The Margins of Medieval Art*. Cambridge, Mass.: Harvard University Press, 1992.

Campbell, Jackson J. "Some Aspects of Meaning in Anglo-Saxon Art and Literature." *Annuale Mediaevale* 15 (1974), 5–45.

Cassidy, Brendan, ed. *The Ruthwell Cross. Papers from the Colloquium Sponsored by the Index of Christian Art, Princeton University, 8 December 1989*. Princeton, N.J.: Princeton University Press, 1992.

Caws, Mary Ann. *Reading Frames in Modern Fiction*. Princeton, N.J.: Princeton University Press, 1985.

Chadwick, Hector M. *The Heroic Age*. Cambridge: Cambridge University Press, 1912.

Chaplan, Rosemary. "A Comparison Between the Junius 11 Adam and Eve Sequence and the Same Sequence in the San Marco Mosaics and Several Touronian Bibles." Unpublished essay. University of Toronto, 1985.

Clemoes, Peter. "Action in *Beowulf* and Our Perception of it." In *Old English Poetry: Essays on Style*. Ed. Daniel G. Calder. Berkeley, Calif.: University of California Press 1979, pp. 147–68.

———. "Mens absentia cogitans in *The Seafarer* and *The Wanderer*." In *Medieval Literature and Civilization: Studies in Memory of G.N. Garmonsway*. Ed. D. Pearsall and D. A. Waldron. London: Athlone Press, 1969, pp. 62–77.

Conner, Patrick W. *Anglo-Saxon Exeter: A Tenth-century Cultural History*, Studies in Anglo-Saxon History, vol. 4. Woodbridge, Suffolk: Boydell, 1993.

Cook, A. S. "Notes on the Ruthwell Cross," *PMLA* 17 (1902), 367–90.

Crowne, David K. "The Hero on the Beach: An Example of Composition by Theme in Anglo-Saxon Poetry." *Neuphilologische Mitteilungen* 61 (1960), 362–72.

Culler, Jonathan. *On Deconstruction: Theory and Criticism after Structuralism*. Ithaca, N.Y.: Cornell University Press, 1982.

———. "Towards a Theory of Non-Genre Literature." In *Surfiction: Fiction Now . . . and Tomorrow*. Ed. Raymond Federman. Chicago: Swallow Press, 1975, pp. 255–62.

Davis, Whitney. "Replication and Depiction in Paleolithic Art." *Representations* 19 (1987), 111–47.

Derrida, Jacques. *The Truth in Painting*. Trans. Geoff Bennington and Ian McLeod. Chicago: University of Chicago Press, 1987.

———. "Structure, Sign, and Play in the Human Sciences." In his *Writing and Difference*. Trans. Alan Bass. Chicago: University of Chicago Press, 1978, pp. 278–95.

Dharmaraj, Glory. *"Beowulf* and Bakhtin: A Study in the Interplay of Voices." Twenty-third International Congress on Medieval Studies, Western Michigan University, Kalamazoo, Mich., 7 May 1988.

Dickens, Bruce, and Alan S. C. Ross, eds. *The Dream of the Rood*, 4th ed. London: Methuen, 1954.

Diller, Hans-Jürgen. "Contiguity and Similarity in the Beowulf Digressions." *Medieval Studies Conference*. Ed. W. D. Bald and H. Weinstock. Frankfurt and New York: Peter Lang, 1984, pp. 71–83.

Doane, Mary Ann. "The Voice in the Cinema: The Articulation of Body and Space." *Yale French Studies* 60 (1980), 33–50.

Dunning, T. P., and A. J. Bliss, eds. *The Wanderer*. London: Methuen, 1969.

Dynes, Wayne. "Imago Leonis." *Gesta* 20:1 (1981), 35–41.

Earl, James W. "Christian Tradition in the Old English *Exodus.*" *Neuphilologische Mitteilungen* 71 (1970), 541–70.

———. "The Typological Structure of *Andreas.*" In *Old English Literature in Context: Ten Essays*. Ed. J. D. Niles. Cambridge and Totowa, NJ: D. S. Brewer/ Rowman and Littlefield, 1980, pp. 66–89.

Eliason, Norman E. "The 'Improvised Lay' in *Beowulf.*" *Philological Quarterly* 31 (1952), 171–79.

Farrell, Robert T. "Reflections on the Iconography of the Ruthwell and Bewcastle Crosses." In *Sources of Anglo-Saxon Culture*. Ed. Paul E. Szarmach. Studies in Medieval Culture 20, Kalamazoo, Mich., Medieval Institute Publications, Western Michigan University, 1986, pp. 357–76.

———, ed. *Daniel and Azarias*. London, 1974.

Finnegan, Ruth. *Literacy and Orality: Studies in the Technology of Communication*. Oxford and New York: Blackwell, 1988.

———. *Oral Poetry: Its Nature, Significance, and Social Context*. Cambridge: Cambridge University Press, 1977.

Fleischman, Suzanne. "Philology, Linguistics, and the Discourse of the Medieval Text." *Speculum* 65:1 (1990), 19–37.

Foley, John Miles. *Immanent Art: From Structure to Meaning in Traditional Oral Epic*. Bloomington, Ind.: Indiana University Press, 1991.

———. "Orality, Textuality, Interpretation." In A. N. Doane and Carol Braun Pasternack, eds. *Vox Intexta: Orality and Textuality in the Middle Ages*. Madison, Wisc.: University of Wisconsin Press, 1991, pp. 34–45.

————. *The Singer of Tales in Performance*. Bloomington, Ind.: Indiana University Press, 1995.

————. "Texts That Speak to Readers Who Hear: Old English Poetry and the Languages of Oral Tradition." In Allen Frantzen, ed. *Speaking Two Languages: Traditional Disciplines and Contemporary Theory in Medieval Studies*. Albany, NY: State University of New York Press, 1991, pp. 141–56.

————. *Traditional Oral Epic: The Odyssey, Beowulf, and the Serbo-Croatian Return Song*. Berkeley, Calif.: University of California Press, 1990.

Frank, Roberta. "Some Uses of Paronomasia in Old English Scriptural Verse." *Speculum* 47 (1972), 207–26.

Frantzen, Allen. "The Archaeology of Deconstruction and the Study of Medieval Sources." New Approaches in Medieval Studies Symposium, Centre for Medieval Studies, Toronto, 29 October 1988.

————. *Desire for Origins: New Language, Old English, and Teaching the Tradition*. New Brunswick, N.J., and London: Rutgers University Press, 1990.

————, ed. *Speaking Two Languages: Traditional Disciplines and Contemporary Theory in Medieval Studies*. Albany, NY: State University of New York Press, 1991.

Frantzen, Allen J., and Charles L. Venegoni. "The Desire for Origins: An Archaeology of Anglo-Saxon Studies," *Style* 20:2 (1986), 142–56.

Gadamer, Hans-Georg. "Rhetoric, Hermeneutics, and the Critique of Ideology: Metacritical Comments on *Truth and Method*." In Kurt Mueller-Vollmer, ed. *The Hermeneutics Reader*. New York: Continuum, 1989, pp. 274–92. Trans. of *Theorie Diskussion: Hermeneutik und Ideologiekritik*, Frankfurt a/M: Suhrkamp, 1971.

————. *Truth and Method*. New York: Crossroad, 1982. Trans. of *Wahrheit und Methode*. Tübingen: Mohr, 1960.

Gage, John. "A Dissertation on St. Æthelwold's Benedictional." *Archaeologia* 24 (1832).

Genette, Gerard. "Modern Mimology: The Dream of a Poetic Language." Trans. Thais E. Morgan. *PMLA* 104 (1989), 202– 14.

Gneuss, Helmut. "The Origin of Standard Old English and Æthelwold's School at Winchester." *Anglo-Saxon England* 1 (1972), 63–83.

Greenfield, Stanley. A *Critical History of Old English Literature*. New York: New York University Press, 1965.

————. "The Formulaic Expression of the Theme of 'Exile' in Anglo-Saxon Poetry." *Speculum* 30 (1955), 200–206. Rpt. in *Essential Articles for the Study of Old English Poetry*. Ed. J. B. Bessinger, Jr., and S. J. Kahrl. Hamden, Conn.: Archon Books, 1968, pp. 352–62.

——. "Min, Sylf, and 'Dramatic Voices in *The Wanderer* and *The Seafarer*.'" *Journal of English and Germanic Philology* 68 (1969), 212–20.

——. "The Old English Elegies." In *Continuations and Beginnings: Studies in Old English Literature*. Ed. E. G. Stanley. London: Thomas Nelson and Sons, 1966, pp. 142–75.

——. "*The Wanderer*: A Reconsideration of Theme and Structure." *Journal of English and Germanic Philology* 50 (1951), 451–65.

Greenfield, Stanley, and Daniel Calder. *A New Critical History of Old English Literature*. New York: New York University Press, 1986.

Healey, A. DiPaolo, and Richard L. Venezky. *A Microfiche Concordance to Old English*. Toronto: Centre for Medieval Studies, University of Toronto, 1980.

Heath, Stephen. "Lessons from Brecht." *Screen* 15:2 (1974), 103–28.

——. *Questions of Cinema*. Bloomington, Ind.: Indiana University Press, 1981.

Hermann, John P. *Allegories of War: Language and Violence in Old English Poetry*. Ann Arbor, Mich.: University of Michigan Press, 1989.

Hieatt, Constance B. "Dream Frame and Verbal Echo in *The Dream of the Rood*." *Neuphilologische Mitteilungen* 72 (1971), 251–63.

Higley, Sarah Lynn. *Between Languages: The Uncooperative Text in Early Welsh and Old English Nature Poetry*. University Park, Pa.: Penn State Press, 1993.

Hollowell, Ida Masters. "On the Identity of the Wanderer." In *The Old English Elegies: New Essays in Criticism and Research*. Ed. Martin Green. Rutherford, NJ and London: Fairleigh Dickinson University Press/Associated University Presses, 1983, pp. 82–95.

Huppé, Bernard F. "The Wanderer: Theme and Structure." *Journal of English and Germanic Philology* 42 (1943), 516–38.

Hutcheon, Linda. *A Poetics of Postmodernism*. New York: Routledge, 1988.

Irvine, Martin. "Anglo-Saxon Literary Theory Exemplified in Old English Poems: Interpreting the Cross in *The Dream of the Rood* and *Elene*." *Style* 20:2 (1986), 157–181.

Jespersen, Otto. *Growth and Structure of the English Language*. 10th ed. Oxford: Blackwell, 1982.

Kelly, Susan. "Anglo-Saxon Lay Society and the Written Word." In *The Uses of Literacy in Early Medieval Europe*. Ed. Rosamond McKitterick. Cambridge: Cambridge University Press, 1990, pp. 36–62.

Kennedy, Alan. "The Thinking of Criticism." *University of Toronto Quarterly* 56 (1987), 443–51.

Kennedy, Charles W. *The Cædmon Poems*. London and New York: George Routledge and Sons, 1916; rpr. Gloucester, Mass: Peter Smith, 1965.

Ker, Neil R. *Catalogue of Manuscripts Containing Anglo-Saxon*. Oxford: Clarendon
Press, 1957.

Kintgen, Eugene R. "Echoic Repetition in Old English Poetry, Especially *The
Dream of the Rood*." *Neuphilologische Mitteilungen* 75 (1974), 202–23.

Kitzinger, Ernst. *Early Medieval Art*. Revised ed. Bloomington, Ind.: Indiana University Press, 1983.

Klinck, Anne L. *The Old English Elegies: A Critical Edition and Genre Study*.
Montreal and Kingston: McGill-Queen's University Press, 1992.

Lacan, Jacques. *Ecrits: a Selection*. Trans. Alan Sheridan. London: Tavistock, 1977.

Lancaster, Lorraine. "Kinship in Anglo-Saxon Society." *British Journal of Sociology* 9 (1958), 230–49 and 359–77.

Lerer, Seth. *Literacy and Power in Anglo-Saxon England*. Lincoln, Neb., and London: University of Nebraska Press, 1991.

Leslie, R. F. *The Wanderer*. Manchester: Manchester University Press, 1966.

Lévi-Strauss, Claude. *The Savage Mind*. Chicago: University of Chicago Press,
1966.

Lewis, Suzanne. "Sacred Calligraphy: The Chi Rho Page in the Book of Kells."
Traditio 36 (1980), 139–59.

Leyerle, John. "The Interlace Structure of *Beowulf*." *University of Toronto Quarterly* 37 (1967), 1–17.

Lord, Albert B. *The Singer of Tales*. Cambridge, Mass.: Harvard University Press,
1969; rpr. New York: Atheneum, 1978.

Loyn, H. R. "Kinship in Anglo-Saxon England." *Anglo-Saxon England* 3 (1974),
197–209.

Macherey, Pierre. *A Theory of Literary Production*. Trans. Geoffrey Wall. London:
Routledge and Kegan Paul, 1978.

Magoun, Francis P. "Oral-Formulaic Character of Anglo-Saxon Narrative Poetry."
Speculum 28 (1953), 446–67.

McEntire, Sandra. "The Devotional Context of the Cross Before A.D. 1000." In
Sources of Anglo-Saxon Culture. Ed. Paul E. Szarmach. Studies in Medieval
Culture 20, Kalamazoo, Mich., Medieval Institute Publications, Western
Michigan University, 1986, pp. 345–56.

McKitterick, Rosamund. *The Carolingians and the Written Word*. Cambridge:
Cambridge University Press, 1989.

——. *The Uses of Literacy in Early Modern Europe*. Cambridge: Cambridge University Press, 1990.

Metz, Christian. "The Imaginary Signifier." Trans. Ben Brewster. *Screen* 16:20 (1975), 14–76. Rpt. in his *The Imaginary Signifier: Psychoanalysis and the Cinema*. Trans. Celia Britton et al. Bloomington, Ind.: Indiana University Press, 1982, pp. 1–98.

Meyvaert, Paul. "An Apocalypse Panel on the Ruthwell Cross." In *Medieval and Renaissance Studies*. Ed. Frank Tirro, Durham, N.C., 1982, pp. 3–32.

Michelfelder, Diane P., and Richard E. Palmer, eds. *Dialogue and Deconstruction: The Gadamer-Derrida Encounter*. Albany, N.Y.: State University of New York Press, 1989.

Nelson, Marie. "The Paradox of Silent Speech in the Exeter Book Riddles." *Neophilologus* 62 (1978), 609–15.

——. "The Rhetoric of the Exeter Book Riddles." *Speculum* 49 (1974), 421–40.

Nichols, Stephen G. "Introduction: Philology in a Manuscript Culture." *Speculum* 65:1 (1990), 1–10.

Ó Carragáin, Éamonn. "Christ over the Beasts and the Agnus Dei: Two Multivalent Panels on the Ruthwell and Bewcastle Crosses." In *Sources of Anglo-Saxon Culture*. Ed. Paul E. Szarmach. Studies in Medieval Culture 20, Kalamazoo, Mich., Medieval Institute Publications, Western Michigan University, 1986, pp. 377–403.

——. "The Ruthwell Crucifixion Poem in Its Iconographic and Liturgical Contexts." *Peritia. Journal of the Medieval Academy of Ireland* 6–7 (1987–88), 1–71.

——. "Seeing, Reading, Singing the Ruthwell Cross: Vernacular Poetry, Old Roman Liturgy, Implied Audience." *Medieval Europe 1992, Prepublished Papers* vol. 7, *Art and Symbolism*, pp. 91–96.

O'Keeffe, Katherine O'Brien. "Orality and the Developing Text of *Cædmon's Hymn*." In her *Visible Song: Transitional Literacy in Old English Verse*. Cambridge Studies in Anglo-Saxon England, vol. 4. Cambridge: Cambridge University Press, 1990, pp. 23–46.

——. "The Written Remembered: Residual Orality and the Question of Sources." Twenty-third International Congress on Medieval Studies, Western Michigan University, Kalamazoo, Mich., 6 May 1988.

Ong, Walter. *Orality and Literacy: The Technologizing of the Word*. London: Methuen, 1982.

Opland, Jeff. *Anglo-Saxon Oral Poetry*. New Haven, Conn., and London: Yale University Press, 1980.

Orton, Peter. "The Technique of Object-Personification in *The Dream of the Rood* and a Comparison with the Old English Riddles." *Leeds Studies in English* 11 (1980), 1–18.

Overing, Gillian. *Language, Sign, and Gender in Beowulf.* Carbondale and Edwardsville, Ill.: Southern Illinois University Press, 1990.

Page, R. I. *An Introduction to English Runes.* London: Methuen, 1973.

——. "Language and Dating in Old English Inscriptions." *Anglia* 77 (1959), 385–406.

Parkes, M. B. "The Literacy of the Laity." *The Medieval World.* Ed. David Daiches and Anthony Thorlby. Literature and Western Civilization, vol. 2. London: Aldus, 1973, pp. 555–77.

Pasternack, Carol Braun. "Anonymous Polyphony and *The Wanderer*'s Textuality." *Anglo-Saxon England* 20 (1991), 99–122.

——. "Stylistic Disjunctions in *The Dream of the Rood.*" *Anglo-Saxon England* 13 (1984), 167–86.

Pope, John C. "Dramatic Voices in *The Wanderer* and *The Seafarer.*" In *Franciplegius: Medieval and Linguistic Studies in Honor of Francis Peabody Magoun, Jr..* Ed. J. B. Bessinger, Jr., and R. P. Creed. New York: New York University Press, 1965, pp. 164–93. Rpt. in *Essential Articles for the Study of Old English Poetry.* Ed. J. B. Bessinger, Jr., and S. J. Kahrl. Hamden, Conn.: Archon Books, 1968, pp. 533–70.

——. "Second Thoughts on the Interpretation of *The Seafarer.*" *Anglo-Saxon England* 3 (1974), 75–86.

Renoir, Alain. *A Key to Old Poems: The Oral-Formulaic Approach to the Interpretation of West-Germanic Verse.* University Park, Pa., and London: Pennsylvania State University Press, 1988.

——. "The Old English *Ruin*: Contrastive Structure and Affective Impact." In *The Old English Elegies: New Essays in Criticism and Research.* Ed. Martin Green. Rutherford, NJ, and London: Fairleigh Dickinson University Press/ Associated University Presses, 1983, pp. 148–73.

——. "Old English Formulas and Themes as Tools for Contextual Interpretation." In *Modes of Interpretation in Old English Literature.* Ed. Phyllis R. Brown, Georgia R. Crampton, and Fred C. Robinson. Toronto: University of Toronto Press, 1986, pp. 65–79.

Richman, Gerald. "Speaker and Speech Boundaries in *The Wanderer.*" *Journal of English and Germanic Philology* 81 (1982), 469–79.

Ricouer, Paul. *Interpretation Theory. Discourse and the Surplus of Meaning.* Fort Worth, Texas: Texas Christian University Press, 1976.

———. *Time and Narrative*, vol. 2. Trans. Kathleen McLaughlin and David Pellauer. Chicago: University of Chicago Press, 1984.

Robinson, Fred. "Artful Ambiguities in the Old English 'Book-Moth' Riddle." In *Anglo-Saxon Poetry: Essays in Appreciation*. Ed. Lewis E. Nicholson and Dolores W. Frese. South Bend, Ind.: Notre Dame University Press, 1975, pp. 355–62.

Robinson, Fred C. *Beowulf and the Appositive Style*. Knoxville, Tenn.: University of Tennessee Press, 1985.

Rosier, James. "Generative Composition in *Beowulf*." *English Studies* 58 (1977), 193–203.

Roy, Gabrielle. *The Road Past Altamont*. Trans. Joyce Marshall. Toronto: McClelland and Stewart, 1976.

Schapiro, Meyer. "On Some Problems in the Semiotics of Visual Art: Field and Vehicle in Image-Signs." *Semiotica* 1 (1969), 223–42.

Shippey, T. A. "Wisdom and Experience: The Old English 'Elegies.'" In his *Old English Verse*. London: Hutchinson and Co., 1972, pp. 53–79.

Silverman, Hugh J. *Textualities: Between Hermeneutics and Deconstruction*. New York and London: Routledge, 1994.

Silverman, Kaja. *The Subject of Semiotics*. Oxford: Oxford University Press, 1983.

Stanley, Eric. *A Collection of Papers with Emphasis on Old English Literature*. Publications of the Dictionary of Old English, vol. 3. Toronto: University of Toronto Press, 1987, pp. 170–91.

Stock, Brian. *The Implications of Literacy: Written Language and Models of Interpretation in the Eleventh and Twelfth Centuries*. Princeton: Princeton University Press, 1983.

———. "Medieval Literacy, Linguistic Theory, and Social Organization." *New Literary History* 16:1 (1984), 13–29.

Swanton, Michael J., ed. *The Dream of the Rood*. Manchester: Manchester University Press, 1970.

Timmer, Benno J. "The Elegiac Mood in Old English Poetry." *English Studies* 24 (1942), 33–44.

Trautman, Moritz, and A.E.H. Swaen. "The Anglo-Saxon Horn Riddles." *Neophilologus* 26 (1941), 298–302.

Whitelock, Dorothy. *The Audience of Beowulf*. Oxford: Clarendon Press, 1951.

Williamson, Craig, ed. *The Old English Riddles of the Exeter Book*. Chapel Hill, N.C.: University of North Carolina Press, 1977.

Wilson, David M. *The Bayeux Tapestry*. London: Thames and Hudson, 1985.

———. *Anglo-Saxon Art: From the Seventh Century to the Norman Conquest*. Woodstock, N.Y.: The Overlook Press, 1984.

Woolf, Rosemary. *"The Wanderer, The Seafarer*, and the Genre of Planctus." In *Anglo-Saxon Poetry: Essays in Appreciation*. Ed. Lewis E. Nicholson and Dolores W. Frese. Notre Dame, Ind.: University of Notre Dame Press, 1975, pp. 192–207.

Wormald, Francis. *The Benedictional of St. Æthelwold*. London: Faber and Faber, 1959.

———. "The Uses of Literacy in Anglo-Saxon England and Its Neighbours." *Transactions of the Royal Historical Society* 5th Series 27 (1977), 95–114.

Zumthor, Paul. *Oral Poetry: An Introduction*. Theory and History of Literature, vol. 70. Trans. Kathryn Murphy-Judy. Minneapolis: University of Minnesota Press, 1990. Originally published as *Introduction à la poésie orale*. Paris: Editions du Seuil, 1983.

———. "The Text and the Voice." *New Literary History* 16:1 (1984), 67–92.

Index

Ælfric, address to reader, 38; *Grammar*, 89
Æthelwold, bishop of Winchester, 89; "Benedictional", 60
Alberti's *De Pictura*, 19
Alfred, preface to *Pastoral Care*, 38, 113–114
Alfred jewel, 48
Andreas, formulaic phrases in, 94; word-hoard in, 93
Anglo-Saxon studies, and critical theory, 1–2, 13–15, 114–116, 117n3
audience, of poetry, 2, 38, 90–91, 104, 107–109, 111, 115, 126n46. See also *Beowulf*, audience of; *Cædmon's Hymn*, audience of; community, as audience of poetry; reading; Ruthwell cross, audience of; *Wanderer*, audience of
author, concept of, 1–2, 12, 77, 84, 107, 111–112

Bakhtin, Mikhail, 84–85, 105–106
Bal, Mieke, 76–77
Barthes, Roland, 1, 2, 19, 96–97, 100, 101
Bartlett, Adeline, 11, 70, 78, 83, 85
Battle of Brunanburh, "beasts of battle" in, 94; formulaic phrases in, 94; variation in, 95–96, 101
Bäuml, Franz, 91, 111–112
Bede. See *Cædmon's Hymn*
Belsey, Catherine, 12, 43
Benjamin, Walter, 13, 73
Benveniste, Emile, 43
Beowulf, audience of, 76, 81, 127n49; and *Daniel*, 73; digressions in, 10, 75–79, 81–

82, 100–101, 115; and *Dream of the Rood*, 73; formulaic themes in, 111; interjections in, 86; intertextuality of, 38–39, 74–75, 80–81; methods of interpreting, 1, 13–14; narrative frames of, 10, 73–75, 79–82, 114; oral tradition in, 91, 103; stories within story, 10–11, 73–82, 114; temporality in, 77, 81–82; verbal repetition in, 83; vocabulary of, 92; voice in, 77–78; wordhoard in, 93–94
Bewcastle cross, 52
binary categories, 3, 5, 10, 44–47, 60, 65–66, 79, 104, 106, 115, 130n68, 146n38
Bliss, Alan J., 28
Bonjour, Adrien, 76, 95, 111
bricoleur, Anglo-Saxon poet as, 92–95, 112
Broderick, H. R., 60
Brooks, Peter, 73
Brussels cross, 48
Bryson, Norman, 19

Cædmon's Hymn, 103–106; audience of, 105
cavepainting, 63, 65, 102, 112, 146–147n42
Caws, Mary Ann, 70, 81
Chadwick, H. M., 75
Christ II, formulaic phrases in, 94
cinema theory, 18, 20, 37, 39, 122n11, 126n43
community, as audience of poetry, 75, 103, 116, 127n48, 127–128n51; identity in relation to, 35–40, 47, 52–53
Cynewulf, 85–86

163